SUCCESS
COMES IN CANS
FAILURE
COMES IN CAN'TS

by
Eugene Anthony Calvano

Printed and bound in the United States of America

INTRODUCTION

I was born in 1924 and I celebrated my 92nd birthday in January of this year with my wife of 66 years, Gloria. We had four children, Annie, Peter, Dominick and Mary. Our dear Lord called our oldest son Pete home in January of 2015. To those of you who have lost one of your children, you can understand how heartbreaking this can be. There is no way to explain the hurt when you see one of your loved ones leave this world at the age of 62, while you're at the age of 92. As the Good Book says, God's ways are not our ways. We were also blessed with 13 grandchildren, 23 great-grandchildren, and when we lost our brother Al and his lovely wife, Rose, we became guardian for five of their children. We called them "God's Blessings."

Why did I decide to write a book? I had a full life. I must say the majority of it was not of the ordinary. You name it, and I can truthfully say to you I've been there; I found that, I saw that, I did that, I was there once. The list can go on and on and in all humility, I lived a life with loads of excitement, good times, weird times, hard times, really tough times along with all the other different phases of life that one could encounter. I did some teaching, but I did much more learning the hard way. A great deal of my learning came from the public at large. Since I worked mostly in sales, management, as a contract worker, business owner, farm manager, and freight handler, I learned at an early age that life is what you make it. Or to put it another way, *You can't crack walnuts by hammering them with mushrooms.* As you read on in my book you will note that I use many clichés. I always like to make my point to those I am speaking to as real as possible. For example: *no guts, no sausage,* or *Why not go out on a limb? That's where the fruit is.*

I have no idea how long it will take me to write this story of my life but if I follow my usual achievement pattern it should not be a very long time. One of the things that comes to my mind is I will soon be 93 years old and time is against me, so I don't have much choice but to move along as quickly as possible. I don't even buy green bananas at my age.

This concludes the introduction to my book entitled SUCCESS COME IN CANS - FAILURE COMES IN CAN'TS. In my words, the best way to find the meaning of the title is as follows: I always kept a vision of my real desires in front of me. I always tried to achieve excellence and the unusual. I always kept my hopes up. I have a positive attitude about my thoughts, visions and their success. I focused on my vision and I made certain that I gave plenty of food for growth.

Chapter 1
MY BELOVED FAMILY

In each chapter of my book I will discuss in depth various incidents that will be related to my family, friends, education, work, and in general, my life experiences. I've tried to keep the chapters in chronological order but most important to me were the experiences in my life at the various times of life along with the plans and strategies and staying power to achieve the desired results. I was told by many folks that my life was so full of happenings that I should write a book.

One of my nieces, the child of my brother Al and his wife Rose, whom we became guardian of, goes by the name of Joni, proposed to me: Uncle Gene, I will assist you in putting together a book about your life. I said to myself, this is too good to pass up. Joni is an attorney, a journalist, a writer and then some and she did this all on her own. So here I am writing the book about my life and Joni is giving me a big league hand.

My first chapter is about my family life and what a blessing that is. Lots of love, discipline, honesty, loyalty, sympathy, devotion, respect, obedience and last but not least faith in God and one another. The sequence of events may not always be in order, nor will this story book appear to you as most normal storybooks would. But keep this in mind; it took me forever to get out of the eighth grade, so please give me a break.

Being that I am in the December of my years, I thought it only fitting to share my thoughts, feelings and memories about my loved ones, to fulfill their request. Before I do, let me first give thanks for the many blessings in my life. To my dear Lord Jesus, who has been so gracious, kind, understanding, compassionate and forgiving to me. For without his love and guidance throughout my life, I may have made a mess of things. He came to my rescue more times than I care to mention.

Let me begin by saying God blessed me with the best parents in the world. They devoted their time, talent and treasure in preparing and teaching me what I needed to know to become a good human being, so I might better serve God and my fellow man, thereby making life worth living. Those were the days when, in raising children, the basics came first. Please, thank you, obedience, honesty, responsibility and respect for others. Soccer, baseball, football, etc., if time allowed, came later.

My folks were very understanding when it came to allowing us time for entertainment and fun. On Saturday mornings, if money allowed, we were given five cents to go to the movies to watch Tom Mix at the local theater. We were also given time to play sports, but again as I mentioned earlier, first things first. You must remember I was raised during the Greatest Depression of all times, but we did what we had to do with regards to responsibilities, and we still found some time to amuse ourselves with our favorite ways of doing so, each to his own liking.

We played games like kick-the-can, hide-and-seek, and baseball on the street. Auto traffic was not one of our major problems in those days.

As for entertainment, in those days there was no radio; we didn't own our first Philco radio until 1935. It was a good part of our entertainment listening to Benny Goodman on the Camel Caravan, The Shadow, Jack Benny and his famous words, "Jell-O again, folks?" We were able to mix in some Westerns and Little Orphan Annie. I still remember the Little Orphan Annie theme song. It went like this: "Who's that little chatterbox, the one with pretty auburn locks. Who could it be, it's Little Orphan Annie, always wearing a sunny smile, now wouldn't it be worthwhile, if you could be like Little Orphan Annie, bright eyes, cheeks of rosy red, there's a glow of health and happiness handy. If you want to know, "arf," says Sandy, always wear a sunny smile, now wouldn't it be worthwhile, if you could be like Little Orphan Annie."

Then there were my 3 brothers and 2 sisters who made my life full of love and fun. Together we learned what the words "share" and "respect" meant to life itself. I learned from my siblings and from my parents that the word "I" had very little meaning when you placed it next to the words *"we"* or *"us"*. Family standards seem to have left the scene today. Too much emphasis on "I" rather than on "we or us." Love is to be shared; it is not something that we keep as our own personal possession. We seem to have forgotten about the word dignity.

I will be inserting copies of letters from my mother as well as some of my own, throughout my book. At this point I would like to insert a letter from my mother. It was written in Italian and translated by my sister-in-law, Mary (may she rest in peace). After you have read it, I think you will understand why I so dearly loved this very precious lady that I call my mother. Incidentally, the letter was written in 1962, just prior to the celebration of Mom and Dad's 50th Wedding Anniversary. Mom and Dad were married for 61 years.

My Mother's Letter Dated May 1962

I am writing these few lines to all my children and my daughters-in-laws and sons-in-law, that if God willing he will give me the grace to celebrate my 50th wedding anniversary. The most happy thing for me is to be together with all my family and all of us to go to Mass and receive Holy Communion together, and your father and I will be very happy if our dear Lord will help us reach this day.

I would also like two bouquets of flowers, one for the Sacred Heart and one for the Blessed Mother.

Of you, I only ask that we are all together to receive Holy Communion and this my beautiful gift that I desire, nothing else. I pray to our Lord that I will receive this gift and to endure such happiness to be all together.

To all of you, I wish good health and that our Lord will keep you all happy during your life and to always have a strong faith in God like I have had. I pray to God for patience and strong faith. Love each other and ask only for God's help to save your soul and good health and God will watch over you and will provide all your needs.

If you pass your life like I did, peaceful, I am sure you will be happy like we are. We are so happy that we have raised a good family, all very respectful and intelligent and very affectionate toward us, more than this grace, we cannot ask for. I feel like I am the richest person in the world.

God has given me a wonderful family that they all have strong faith in God and have love for each other. Please, don't ever lose hope and faith in God, for whoever has faith and love has everything.

May God bless all of you, with all of your families. This letter is for all of you to keep and if God takes me before my anniversary, do the same as if I was there.

I wish all you good luck and a long and happy life.

Your Mother, Rose

As a tack on to my mother's letter, studies have shown that good close relationships produce good health and good brains during your life and the ability to overcome illness more rapidly. In other words, loving people and sharing yourself with others, being on friendly terms, avoiding unfriendly relations are good for the mind and the body. Whereas the opposite has a tendency to produce unhappiness, illness and a shorter life. We must always remember that God gave us a choice, it's ours to make, the easy way or the hard way, the positive way or the negative way. We either walk toward HIM or away from HIM. We may choose God's way or the other way.

Then God went ahead and said, "Gene, here are your children, Annie, Peter, Dominick and Mary." Boy, talk about being on cloud nine each time one of them came into the world. You could always find us on cloud nine! We were always so proud to take them out to family affairs, church, restaurants, you name it, they were all such well- behaved and well-mannered children. It made us very proud. People would take the time to stop and tell us what beautiful and well-mannered children they all were. It was fun and an honor to be called their parents. I will share a few thoughts about each one of them as I recall them as children and as adults. All different in many ways but all of them have what I call the main ingredient, love for one another and love of their fellow man. They all continue to hold on to the most important ingredients as they move on with their lives to this date.

Before I share further thoughts, feelings and memories about all our children, and I say all because I want to include the five children we were awarded guardianship over. They were the children of my dearest brother Al and lovely, lovely wife Rose, but that will be discussed in a future chapter.

Now let me share with you the greatest event in my life. It was the happiest, biggest, best, most joyful day of my life. It was the day I met my little "Angel from heaven", my wife Gloria. I have always believed that you get out of life what you put into it, and to go a step further, you need to have a picture in your mind. A clear picture of the dream or wish that you expect to receive. l always prayed to mama Mary, Mother of Christ for the kind of girl I would like to take for my wife. Similar to some of the women in our family who I thought quite a bit of, my mom, my sister-in-law Mary, my sister-in-law Rose, my sister Teresa and my cousin Elsie. They were the kind of women who made a house a home and they were adored by their husbands and children. They were always kind, loving, understanding, compassionate and confident with the right amount of humor to make life laughable. The best part of their character was that it all came natural. They were blessed with gifts from God and they shared their gifts with others, as God has asked us to do.

Back to my dear Gloria, I would have never been able to achieve success in my life without her love and support. Whoever said, "Behind every good man, there is a good woman." I am not implying that I was a good man, what I am trying to say is that I had a beautiful, lovely, confident, good human being for a wife. She was my key motivator on every job I held. Every challenge I had, every illness that struck me, every problem I encountered, every great event, every loss, every gain. In plain words she was and is my everything. I often think out loud at times: no wonder our children are also talented, lovable, respectful and dependable. They are a carbon copy of her.

I recall the time when I told her that my brother Al, after losing his lovely wife, Rose had asked me to promise him I would look after his children if he left this world sooner than I did. In her usual compassionate, timely manner, she said, "Yes," very graciously and very proudly. At this point I think it is worthy to mention that Gloria had a beautiful bringing up. There were only two children in Gloria's family. Gloria had a sister named Dolores and her mom, who was a very gracious lady and was named Mary. Both Gloria's mom and sister have gone on to a better life but they were able to share some good years with our four children before they passed away. Gloria's mom and dad pretty much raised their children as my folks raised us. I never had the pleasure or the opportunity to meet Gloria's dad, Peter. "May he rest in peace." To listen to Gloria speak so proudly and so lovingly of her dad makes me feel as though I knew him and how I WISHED on many events during our lifetime for him to have been there to share our blessed events with us. But you know something, I am certain our loved ones who leave this world before us know what is happening to us in our lives each day.

Marriage is a beautiful thing but it also brings with it many responsibilities, and one wonders how he will handle the situation. Will he be able to meet all obligations as a husband, father, friend, and as a lover, etc? Will my wife and I agree on many issues we will be facing? I must admit it was more than what I had answers for. So I did what I normally do when in doubt. I got on my knees and talked to God about it in my manner. I need your guidance. I just left it up to Him. I trusted Him. I always have and always will. Trust is a beautiful thing for those of you that have not read this in the past. I place it here now for your guidance. FAITH is of the mind, BELIEF is of the will and TRUST is of the heart. So when you say you trust in Jesus, you are telling God: You know, I have a good feeling deep down inside of me, about how much you have done for me, and still continue to help me, in spite of my ungratefulness to you at times.

Back to our children. We had our first child, Annie, exactly one year and one day from the day we were married. I used to tell folks that Annie was born on June 9 and we were married on June 10, but I never mentioned the year. Big joke, ha-ha. Annie was the first of four beautiful children. We were not concerned about having a baby boy or baby girl, we would love whoever God gave us. He gave us little Annie with all her alert qualities, she was a beautiful child with her bright eyes. We knew God had given us a winner. She did well in school, everyone liked her and she was always fun to be around.

I am certain she inherited a lot of her craft talents from her Grandmas; they were both highly talented in the area of sewing, cooking, decorating, craftsmanship, imagination and organizing skills. Annie met a young lad named Jerry Schlosser and after a brief romance they were married in 1970. I recall when Jerry and Annie got married, I said to myself what a man Annie had gotten herself. Muscular, handsome, well-informed, conscientious and a hard worker. Much of Jerry's demeanor is visible in his three sons, their character and their behavior. During the 13 years that they were married they had three beautiful boys, Patrick,

Dominick and Jeremy. They turned out to be three of the greatest guys you ever want to meet. Pat did so well in school that he wound up as school principal at Apple Valley High School and since then has been promoted once again. Dominick is a first-rate plumber, running great jobs from the point of infrastructure to the chrome faucet.

And Jeremy--who would've thought this little guy would turn out to be 6-foot-6 or more and full of wood craftsmanship talent? Now he operates and is part owner of a professional cabinet shop. He makes cabinets of all sorts for home, commercial use, etc. Needless to say, the three boys gave us eight great-grandchildren. These three sons of Annie and Jerry turned out to be three great, great human beings. Annie and Jerry separated ways after 13 years, much to our unhappiness.

Then Annie met Ed Gaunder. They say that God provides and he does because here was Annie raising three boys on her own. Along comes this great guy who was a career man with the Federal Prison System. They saw what they liked in each other and were married in 1985 and they came up with another great guy, a fourth son. Annie and Ed named him John. He too is loaded with talent. First off, he is a great human being, a journeyman plumber, computer technician and is well on the way to a successful job with the City of Hesperia in the line of management.

As for Annie she has done great and she does it all. Business owner, pottery maker, quilt maker, dressmaker, home- decorator, first-class cook including gourmet delicacies. She made a trip to

Burundi, Africa to show folks how to sew and is also a member of a charitable group to raise funds to help the women in Africa find a better way of life. Did I mention that Annie is a great artist also? So we close this portion of our children off with our thanks to God for all their great grandchildren.

Annie's oldest son, Patrick, met up with a very lovely lady named Shannon. They decided on a partnership of marriage and before long they added Ruth and Dominick to our great-grandchildren list. Pat and Shannon spent several years in the Peace Corps prior to and when they came back to America they had a foundation that was as solid as it could be. Pat and Shannon, on their return to California from Eritrea, Africa, had a true understanding of how great a country we live in. Shannon has so much talent and is such a kind, considerate person. Between them, they came up with features in their children like writing, drawing, piano playing, just all kinds of talent.

Dominick married Kristi and they added more great-grandchildren, Trevor, Justin and Travis. It never ceases to amaze me how all the good human features are so well spread throughout our family. I mean real talent, great manners, natural good looks, we have been blessed.

Jeremy and Tiffany fell in love while in high school and started their family early in life. They got the jump on the rest of the gang. They came in with their three jewels, Cody, Alex and Cami. More talent, more beauty and more of that good human feature, love.

Then Gloria and I decided to have another child. It's something we thought about once a year. Gloria was pregnant for the first five years we were married. We had four children and one miscarriage in five years. I recall how happy I was to have our first son. I wanted so much to name him after me but I stepped aside for Gloria's dad. His name was Peter and he deserved it. I recall when we baptized Peter Joseph Calvano, we invited 200 people and rented a hall in Monrovia, California for the event that was one-of-a-kind. As a kid, Pete had lot of determination, compassion, full of mischief and loved school just like his dad did, ha-ha. I recall telling Gloria at an early age in Peter's life not to worry about Pete, that he would always take care of himself and he always did. I saw in Pete so much of myself. Lots of go, plenty of ideas, not a quitter and desire to move forward.

Pete was a self-made man. He had the ingredients to go in any direction he chose. My concern was to be sure he would choose the right direction. Pete had his ups and downs in marriage but he made a name for himself in the business world. He and his first wife Kathy brought Stefani into our world. She is a chip off her dad! Stefani and her husband Bryan are both active in the business world. I always liked Kathy, Pete's first wife. I hated to see them separate. Pete remarried, and the girl he married was another bright spot in Pete's and our lives. Her name was Deidre. They brought little Dusti into our lives. Dusti is a little jewel. She is quiet, calm and reserved with a sense of humor and with kindness of no end. Dusti and

Thomas enjoy operating a successful phone business. Thomas is certainly deserving of Dusti. He is a fine example of a human being and a gentleman, with many home-building talents and other trade specialties.

Who's to say why couples get divorced? We love Pete's wives from past marriages and we could not stand to see them leave our family circle. As I mentioned earlier, marriage is a tremendous responsibility and it needs all you have to make it go. When I say all, I mean love, patience, kindness, love, understanding, love, etc. I once read an article in our daily newspaper about a couple who were married for 89 years and they asked the husband if he could briefly state the reason for their long term marriage. He said, "Yes, it's very simple, you give, you take and you compromise." My, what wise words of wisdom.

On January 3, 2015, my wife, Gloria and I received a phone call from my daughter Annie and her husband, Ed. They called to tell us that our dear son Peter Joseph had suffered a major heart attack and had died. It's the kind of phone call that a father of 91+ doesn't expect. My dear wife Gloria and I never dreamed of seeing of our children leave this world before us.

Pete had nothing but success in his retail food business that he operated out of Los Angeles. Pete had major accounts with chain stores, such as Kroger's, Albertson's, Safeway, and Food 4 Less, which covered most of the major chains throughout the United States.

Pete's Chinese wife named Ying and their two sons, Thomas, five years old and Christopher, approximately 3 months old, were completely devastated, as was our entire family, friends and relatives. Both my wife and I are trying to live with broken hearts and with the help of our blessed Lord Jesus Christ, we shall carry our cross as He carried his cross for us.

We had never seen Peter as happy as he was with his two new sons and they just adored him. I would like to add at this point that Ying has proven to be a beautiful mother, a great lady, very resourceful, very kind, and we just adore her and the boys. I am including in this chapter a copy of the eulogy that I had written at Pete's funeral.

Peter Calvano's Eulogy

My name is Gene Calvano. I am the old block that the chip comes from.

I will have to read what I am going to share with you, because at 91, my memory is not as good as it was at 51.

On behalf of my wife, Gloria and I, Pete's wife, Ying and Pete's children, Thomas, Christopher, Dusti and Stefani, we thank you for your presence here today. You are all very kind.

What can I tell you about our son, Pete? After giving this some thought, I decided it's not what I can tell you about Pete, but rather what do those folks who had personal contact with Pete have to say about him?

I found in one of my books, an article entitled, "One Man's Creed" and I would like to share it with you.

General James Jimmy Doolittle is probably best known for leading an American bombing raid on Tokyo, Japan during World War II.

However, his list of achievements goes far beyond being a military leader.

Doolittle was a boxing champion; Pete was not a boxer but he was a fighter.

Doolittle was a pilot and a stunt pilot; Pete was not a stunt pilot, but he could fly a plane.

Doolittle was an aviation record setter; Pete was not an aviator record setter, but he owned over 100 cars in his lifetime. That's a record!

Doolittle was a scientist; Pete made the produce business his science.

Doolittle was an advisor to Presidents; Pete gave a lot of advice to folks when it was really needed.

The similarity in their human character was not so much the things I just mentioned, but there is much similarity in their relationship with their fellow man.

Doolittle formed the philosophy that every person has been put on this earth to serve his fellow man. It does not matter how he does this. He can build a bridge, paint a picture, invent some labor-saving gadget or run a gas station.

The point is, we should try to leave the earth a better place than we found it.

If we do, life will have been worthwhile. If do not do what we can within our own limitations, we are destined to be unhappy.

Doolittle points out that the key to happiness is found by serving other people. That was our son Pete's philosophy. To exhibit the humility of a truly great person, here is an example. It was characteristics of Doolittle and Pete.

If we can serve others without boasting, we accomplish even a greater achievement. In the process, we are serving God as well.

Love for Pete came from friends, family, relatives, coworkers, strangers, because he loved people.

Here are a couple of samples of Pete's character.

My nephew Sam Calvano heads up our annual family reunion affair. He had called Pete for help on a matter. After his request was fulfilled by Pete, Pete asked Sam, "Is there anything else I can help with?" Sam said, "Yes, send me some money!" He was only kidding. But Pete wasn't, he emailed Sam and inquired, "How much do you need?"

Another example, an email from one of our dear nieces.

Dear Uncle Gene and Aunt Gloria,
I am sending this email just to let you know I am thinking about you constantly and praying that God will hold you close to him as you go through this loss of your dear son, Pete. His life was an example of your love in all its most wonderful aspects. I keep thinking there must be hundreds of people who are grateful to Pete for the many acts of kindness he did for them, that he probably never talked about to anyone else.

He was a person with a deep compassion for people. He never lingered once the inclination to help someone became known to him. He just gave whatever he had. Many of us among the family and friends were beneficiaries of his generosity and kindness. But there must be many more who experienced it and wondered how he could care enough to help them when he had no ties of blood or long-term friendship. Pete was a wonderful, memorable, profoundly kind man, and everyone in our family will miss his smile, his warmth and friendship. You raised a great person. He had all the best qualities of both of you.

God bless you both.

Love, Joni

Thanks Joni.

Pete, we are proud of your performance here on earth. You left earth a better place than you found it. You treated your fellow man with dignity. It is time for us to share your memories within our heart. Though we can't touch, we'll still be near with memories so clear. Pete, you served God well, you earned your reward.

Our thanks once again to each of you and May God Bless You and yours always, in all ways.

After Pete was born then came our third child, Dominick, and there went our knick-knacks, plants in the television planter. With Dom came rock'n roll. He could sit and rock in any chair he sat in.

Dom was also the top employee at Jack-In-The-Box for about two weeks. We call him Dom the drummer, the singer, the comedian, MC, strongest man, he also liked being called Mr. Wonderful. Entertainer Dom can do it all, he was active and I mean active. Whenever we took a trip that involved long rides there would be Annie, Pete and Mary sound asleep but in my rearview mirror I could see Dom rockin-n-rollin.

We were glad to see Dom grow up and get married, as he played the drums every day after school for years. Dom married a very nice girl named Joni and they presented us with Mandy who has Dom's humor and bright mind for business. Dom and Joni's marriage ended rather abruptly. It's unfortunate but these things do occur. Gloria and I just love Mandy's manner and humor. She is a great human being and a great gal.

Dom married Donna and they presented us with little Krissy. Krissy was born without her left hand and forearm; God decided to give her extra mental aptitude, extra drive, extra energy and just about everything a little extra. It didn't bother Krissy to be missing the hand. Between God and mankind she was given prosthesis and went straight up and forward; she does just about what everybody else does. She did great in school, wound up going to Northern Arizona University where she served as the team captain of the snare drum team. Krissy was also president of the Kappa Kappa Psi. For those of you who would like a little hands-on Krissy success, remember these three words, *and then some,* because these are what a person needs to stand out from the others.

Now we talk about our last child. I am sure you heard the saying "last but not least," well that's our Mary. We named her after Mary, her grandma. We also named her after Mary, mother of Jesus, and she has the qualities of both of those Mary's.

Our daughter Mary fell in love in high school with a boy by the name of Peter Dittemore. I still recall coming home early one afternoon and finding Mary talking to Peter in our driveway. After his departure, I asked Mary who was the character with the beard and all the hair. Well, to make it short they continued their relationship all through high school. Mary at the age of 17 and Peter at the age of 19 decided they were ready to get married. First thoughts were, you're too young and so soon out of school, but both Mary and Peter displayed good common sense and they were very intent and serious about getting married.

To date they have been married over 40 years and have three children, David, Faye and Justin, who are happily married and have presented us with another eight great-grandchildren.

David married Tami, who is a special mom with lots of talent. They have four children, Alisa, Ethan, Anthony and Gabriella. Pardon the expression, Tami is a bigwig with a large computer concern. David is in charge of safety at the Federal Prison System in Victorville, California. With God's help they are set on a solid line. They own their own home on 2 ½ acres.

Little Faye used to play a trombone in the front yard where we lived close together in Apple Valley.

She tried hard, but I knew she would never become a trombone player, but it was a good fill-in item at the time. Faye married a great guy by the name of Larry Barber. Larry operates his own business, loves basketball, great husband and a great dad. Faye is very artistic with oil painting, water painting, charcoal sketching, company logos, expert printing. I don't intend to sound boastful but as I've told Faye on more than one occasion, "God has really blessed you, make certain that you thank Him for it." Faye and Larry have two children, Caleb and Gracie. Caleb shows signs of perhaps someday doing work for our blessed Lord and Gracie has a lot of talent; she will probably be able to pick and choose at her discretion.

Justin married a beautiful lady named Daryn and they have two children, Kayleigh and Bryanna. They are both excellent students. Very talented in sports, Bryanna loves soccer and it appears as though Kayleigh is headed for Doctorville. Justin is the general manager of the company that manufactures truck tankers and believe me, he does his job well. As for Daryn, she worked hard and long to become a nurse and since has moved up and is in the upper echelon.

Once when I became ill and exhausted from overwork, upon visiting the doctor his remarks to me were, "Gene, you are exhausted." It is like writing a check with no money in your account. In this case I was given some time off from my job of managing the produce operation for a major chain store in Southern California with 242 stores. It was a serious illness and it took several months to make myself well again. I did and yes I went back to my job and stayed on for another 20 years. My reason for telling you this, during the time I was home with my illness, my little Mary was in the first grade. The best part of my day was to walk her to the school bus and then wait for the school bus to bring her back home. The minute I saw her smiling face my whole world changed. I know that my rest during the time I was off and the medical treatments I received had much to do with my health improvement, but to this day I think my little Mary had a lot to do with my getting well.

Mary will turn 60 years of age this month. She still has a great smile, lots of compassion, lots of love and a great desire to help those in need. Thank God for giving us such beautiful children. My mother used to tell us if you look at the fingers on your hand they are all different in size but yet each one of them is important to you and each one of thcm peiforms a job tor you and each one of them is needed by you. Then she would say, "This is the way it is with a family of children, they are all different but they all have their good points and not so good points. But as parents, it's up to us to bring out the best in them."

God has really gone all out for my wife, Gloria and me. He has blessed us with so many beautiful children, grandchildren, great-grandchildren and the children of my dear brother, Al and his wife, Rose. We have been blessed and we thank him every day, for little did we know on June 10, 1950, our wedding day, that we would someday be the proud parents of so many beautiful children, grandchildren, great-grandchildren.

Having a big family is a beautiful thing. Having a big family that gets along harmoniously is a great, great big beautiful thing. It is really heartwarming to see. When we get together for special occasions it is always a very warm and loving affair, with a mixture of races that consists of white, black, brown, yellow and just about every nationality.

One of my special memories that stands out among many is, I have a grandson for a camping buddy. Mary and Peter's youngest boy, Justin, and I became real camping buddies. We camped every way you can think of. In my 35-foot motorhome, camping in tents, sleeping on the ground, cooking meals from scratch. We were camping buddies for about 10 years. Gloria and I shared much of our time with our family members; we are really family-oriented. To me it brings to mind what a gentleman told me at a young age: if you have strong, loving family, you are blessed. A good family life builds character, builds countries, builds relationships, teaches you how to love, how to respect others with dignity. It teaches you about humility and most of all you concentrate more on "we and us," rather than "me, myself and I."

This concludes the chapter on my family. I will elaborate in another chapter on the five beautiful children that God blessed us with upon the death of my brother and his wife.

In my next chapter I will begin to share my life experiences with you from an early age to the present day. Things happen in life, as you will see, but life still must go on. That is how I arrived at the title to this book. There are some things in life that you can't or shouldn't do and there are some things in life that you can or should do. Things you shouldn't do can cause you problems but you can learn from them and learn to live a better life thereafter. That's why this saying fills the bill so nicely; a setback is an opportunity to begin again more intelligently when the time is right.

Chapter 2
MY EARLY LIFE

I was born long ago and far away in the city of Chicago. They call it the Windy City. I came from a family of six children, four boys and two girls and I was, as they used to call me in those days, "the baby of the family".

For those of you who are not familiar with life in Chicago, let me say this. I loved living in Chicago, particularly during the period between 1924 and 1941. Each neighborhood had its own nationality. Italians, Polish, Irish, Jewish, Hungarian, these were the main nationalities that I grew up with. But let me tell you what I didn't like about Chicago: it's cold in the winter and hot in the summer, sultry in the summer, mosquitoes eat you alive, snow lasts forever in the wintertime and it is extremely difficult to heat a home without a central heating system. I will have more on that later. At any rate, I did enjoy my days in Chicago, and I think it helped me build a good, strong foundation for life in the days ahead.

I learned to speak Italian before I spoke English. My brothers and sisters spoke to me in English, my mom and dad spoke to me in Italian. You know something; you can do so much in life if you just accept the fact that this is the way it's going to be. There is no other way out, at least for the moment, maybe later when you've mastered things, you can change your style or your pattern of living. At any rate, being that I was the baby of the family I got some inside information on the dos and don'ts of family living and I got to see it in live action. That's quite an advantage.

I was last one to start school, so I spent some special time with my dear mother, being the only one home alone with her during the daytime. My mother was quite a seamstress; she made bright fancy dresses, shirts, pants, sheets. The fact is she did an awful lot of crocheting, knitting and was an excellent cook. She was the kind of mom everybody would like to have. As I recall, I was on the floor near the sewing machine and on occasion she would ask me to hold up the material so it would flow nicely through the sewing machine and of course I was also a little errand boy for child preschool days. I recall those days as I watched her sew and cook and do it so wisely, so economically and so accurately. No waste, no haste, just a job well done. I recall one day I had an accident and pooped in my pants. She wasn't terribly upset but I could tell that she wished I was old enough to go to school. Well that day came soon enough, she took me to my first day of school and I caused a big scene. I refused to stay in school and every time she would leave to go I would run after her. After about 10 tries, Ma and the teacher convinced me stay in school. So you will see as the chapters of this book unfold how I had a problem with my school days.

Chapter 3
MY SCHOOL LIFE

I didn't exactly hate school; I think one of the things that annoyed me the most was the mere fact of staying put hour after hour in one seat. I knew the answers to a lot of material and a lot of the material that the teacher shared with us was rather boring at times. I did like to talk a lot and I'm sure I disturbed my teachers with that kind of behavior. I did well in most subjects, history, geography, music, math, or as we called it in those days, arithmetic. Fact of the matter, through most of my life I seldom used a calculator. I would have the answers from memory as others attempted to get the answer on their calculators. I guess you might say I had an overactive mind in school. It was not fulfilling what I desired. So I just kind of put my time in until I got to the eighth grade. I think if I was in school today at 92, I would still be in the eighth grade.

When I finally got out of the eighth grade, my dear beautiful mother said, "Now that you are out of school you must find yourself a job." So I looked around for a job and I found one at a national grocery chain in Chicago and the manager said he could use me in his produce department. It wasn't too long after that when he called me in his office one day and asked if I would like to run this department. As you can imagine, here I am a 16-year-old on the job for about 10 months being offered a manager's position. The irony of the whole thing is this, there were 11 employees in that produce department, the oldest one 42 years old and he was the prior manager. Now, he would be assigned under my management. Needless to say, I was proud of my new position, produce department sales rose to an average of over $2,200.00 a week and those are big-time sales in those days. It was about the year of 1939 or 1940. Potatoes on special sold for 19 cents a peck, carrots on sale sold for 1 cent per bunch, apples 3 pounds for 10 cents. In order to reach $2,200.00 in sales, we had to sell tons and tons of produce.

The manager liked my work so well he would take my mother shopping to his store on Sunday, because the stores were closed on Sunday and he had work to do and he would tell her, "You can shop while I get my work done." To me that was a lot better than school. I was earning $22.00 a week and I was getting plenty of street smarts dealing with the public and learning the produce business.

Incidentally , I failed to mention when I left school not only did my mother tell me to find a job she also said when lunchtime comes around, the potatoes are in the bag underneath the sink, help yourself, peel them. I'm not waiting on you, since you have decided to leave school. As soon as you get a job I once again will serve you. That motivated me to look for a job and let me tell you I found one pretty fast. Long story short, when I got to California I went to a place called the Downey Food Market and asked for a produce job and a gentleman asked if I had any produce experience. I proceeded to tell him "yes", that I had managed a produce department in Chicago for a national chain. He said, "Well good, why don't we do this? Why don't you work for me for one week and I'll pay you what I think you're worth and you let me know if it is agreeable with you or not." There's nothing I can't do if it's in the area of what I like to do. You know the old saying, 80% of the people do not care for the work they do. So one of the secrets of making a good living is to find out what you're good at and go after it. SUCCESS COMES IN CANS, FAILURE COMES IN CAN'TS. Low and behold after one week the gentleman came up to me and offered me $27.50 as a produce clerk whereas in Chicago I was earning $22.00 a week as a manager. I guess this would be a good place to insert, NO GUTS, NO SAUSAGE or HE WHO HESITATES IS LOST.

I realize that this chapter is supposedly about school but since school was not a big part of my life I just wanted to show you, and you will see more of this in the chapters ahead, that I received most of my schooling on the frontlines.

Chapter 4
MY FAMILY RELATIONSHIPS
AND EXPERIENCES

In the first three chapters I shared my thoughts and feelings regarding my family, a bit of my early life and some of my school life. In this next chapter I want to share family member relationships and experiences.

Our dear brother Arthur was stationed in California and happened to be one of the first draftees of World War II. Since Mom and Dad were born in Italy and California seemed so much like Italy to them, especially the climate, and it was a nice place to live, they decided to move there in 1942.

My mom and dad were both from the Italian town of Catanzaro, so needless to say a lot of their customs and ways of life had that Italian flair to them; or in layman's language, "the way they did it in the old country." I'll begin with my dad because I believe he was the most successful with us children regarding work details he assigned to us.

In the next few paragraphs, I will try to explain the things he did with us and for us. Also the many things he had us do for him. He was an excellent provider, a good father and a master at getting his children to carry their share of the overall family work load, which we didn't mind at all, because we grew up with it and it just became a way of life.

I remember asking my dad some questions about his early employment when he first came to America. Things like how many hours a day did he work, how much was he paid? His answer was that he earned a dollar a day. He went to work at 6 a.m. and the day ended whenever the foreman told him to go home. Some days he worked 16 hours. It was in his early days and he worked mostly for a foundry and for the Illinois Central Railroad Company.

Later in life he was employed by Carson Pierie Scott and Company in downtown Chicago. He remained employed there for many years. He never drove a car so it was always a long streetcar ride, approximately 10 to 12 miles, to and from work.

A good portion of our life in Chicago was during the Great Depression. So his earnings were a mere $14.00 per week, and that's how much money we had to pay for rent, food, clothing, medical, and naturally entertainment was out of the picture. My dad had a lot of talent. For example when any of his children's shoes needed soles or heels he had his little shoe repair forms and tools and that saved a lot of money.

Whenever we moved to a new residence my dad always made certain there was an empty lot next door. I do not ever recall his not having a garden during the summertime, which would produce so much good fresh produce like tomatoes, eggplant, green beans, potatoes, beets, bell peppers, Swiss chard, escarole, etc.

He had some friends who were musically inclined. They played guitars, mandolins and had good singing voices. On occasion, on a Sunday afternoon, he would invite them over and all of us kids would sit on the floor and listen to the gentlemen singing Mom and Dad's favorite Italian songs.

Along with the singing there was always the sharing of my dad's homemade red wine and our own special cured homemade Italian sausage and my mom's homemade bread. In those days that was food fit for a king. I loved my dad; he was a hard worker and a very handy man around the house. He loved God, took excellent care of my mom, who had 14 surgeries in her lifetime, and his style of discipline was very effective.

Our entertainment was limited. During the depression, in addition to whatever I have stated up to this point, there were two other items we relied on for fun. One of them was an Italian card game, similar to bridge. It was called Briscola and the other one was an Italian version of Bingo, it was called Tombola. They were both a lot of fun and broke up our hum-drum routine. Sometimes we played them on Sunday afternoons, after my mom's special Sunday dinners that included homemade noodles, Italian meatballs, roast chicken, broccoli for a vegetable and a real good Italian salad that included tomatoes, cucumbers, radishes, garlic, vinegar and salt. The more I write the hungrier I get.

We always ate most of our meals together as a family. My parents always said that mealtime within the family was a sacred time and there was little conversation during the actual consumption of the meal. But after the meal we would sit around and talk about different events that happened that particular day. It is what I would refer to as therapy time; we somehow seem to have lost that in our present day lifestyle. It promotes togetherness, respect, loyalty and love for one another. My mom was the kind of mom that every child dreams about. There are a couple of important things I think need to be said about this beautiful mother of mine. Her schooling consisted of the fourth grade in Italy. No schooling here in America except what she learned from her children. She could read and write Italian. She could read English to a degree and could write very little English, but the one thing she had was wisdom.

As a youngster I wondered how she knew so much and was so helpful to so many. People would come by the house frequently seeking her counseling. As a youngster I couldn't quite digest how she achieved all this with the limited schooling she had attended. Later on, as a young man, I finally realized the one thing she had was a love for God. She loved Jesus, she trusted him and she did her best to live like him. That's when I realized that it was wisdom of which she had an abundance and it came from God. She asked Him for it, she served Him, she loved people, and she was compassionate. When one was in trouble she didn't condemn, she tried to console, encourage and help strengthen their character.

Even though our income was what we called in those days the relief level, my mom was economical, wise and had the ability to prepare a decent meal practically from nothing. God had blessed us. We never once had to call upon help from the relief programs available to the public. On occasion we were offered assistance but Mom politely said, "No thank you, we are in good shape, please pass it on to someone else that may be in more need of it." She did likewise when my grandparents passed away in Italy. Her family wrote to her and informed her that she was entitled to a portion of the inheritance. She very kindly and lovingly wrote back to them and told them that they could take her portion and divide it among themselves because here in America we were all well cared for.

It has been said a family that prays together, stays together. It's not only the prayer that keeps the family together. It is the love for each other, but I'm certain that the prayer brings about the love. I recall so many beautiful family gatherings and not only on holidays. Sunday afternoon picnics at Jackson Park in Chicago. Christmas Eve and New Year's Eve, Thanksgiving and birthdays, they were really sacred times and who made these events blessed? My dear mother, Rose. She is the only person I ever knew who cooked everything well, never followed the recipe but there was a lot of love in that food. When I say food, I mean up to 30 different dishes of different types of food, all done by one person by hand and minus all of today's modern kitchen equipment. But you never saw a finer meal, more beautiful table, happier people or more love in the home then you saw at these gathering.

"To each his own", as they say, but as for me, I certainly think our dear Lord put me upon this earth in middle of a beautiful family. The Great Depression and World War II were on us but they built our character and made us better people. I am happy to be born when I was. God has blessed us.

As I mentioned earlier, my sister Ida was the oldest in the family. She was also my dad's favorite of all the children in our family. I always thought his choice was largely because I didn't learn to read Italian and write Italian, sing Italian songs and in general she had a decent singing voice.

Just a few highlights about Ida, she was the character. Her shopping habits were from another planet. She lived to be 99 years old and during those years, a conservative estimate of the number of trips she made to all types of stores was on the average of three per day. That included Sundays, during part of those 99 years. Her big ambition was taking pictures of families and friends on birthdays, holidays and special occasions. A sunny day could've been a special occasion. I could probably enjoy a much better retirement if I had the money she spent on film developing and postage stamps. When she took a picture, every one, family and friends, relatives would all get a copy. On the envelope would be written the words "DO NOT BEND", so she is the buyer of roles of labels that stated on them "DO NOT BEND."

God bless her, it was her big thing in life and she really enjoyed it. The other thing she was notorious for was returning purchases for various reasons. Most of the time to return would involve exchange of items or a complete money refund. I used to always tell her she would never get an ulcer.

"You don't get ulcers, you give them." So much for Ida, may she rest in peace. God was good to her though because she had the kind of husband that most women dream about. His name was Dominick and a kinder gentleman you would never find. He was kind, gentle, compassionate, understanding, humorous, loved the Lord and in general loved people.

Ida and Dominick had beautiful children. They had four, Mary Jane (God rest her soul). She was beautiful, talented, humorous and was loved by everyone, just like her dad. The second one in line was Rita, beautiful, kind, generous, lovable and always willing to help those in need. Then came Raymond, he was truly a reproduction of his dad, Dominick. You see Ray, you see Dominick and vice versa. Then came Judy. Judy was special in her own way, one might classify her as a deep thinker, outspoken and one who likes to have answers. All in all, these four wonderful children fall in the same category as the rest of our clan, friendly, kind, considerate, helpful for those in need and they praise their God.

There was my brother Dominick and his wife Mary. In our family God blessed all of us children with the nicest spouses. It may seem strange to some people but all of our spouses were Italian and they were Catholic. My mom used to tell us if you marry within your own nationality and your own religion, you eliminate a lot of possible areas of conflict over food, lifestyle and religion, and she was right. It gave us a running start.

Busse was a great guy in his prime. He was over 6 feet tall, about 200 pounds, gentle as a lamb. But you didn't want to upset him. Although I was his little brother, as it turned out later in life, I became more like his big brother. He was an auto mechanic by trade and a good one. He spent many years with the Navy at their missile testing stations here in Southern California. He developed a serious back injury and retired on disability at the age of 42. He played guitar and sang well. He was part of our group. All four of us had a little business in Chicago. Dominick played guitar, Arthur played saxophone, Al played piano and accordion and I played drums. We would play for weddings, parties, special events and we had a lot of fun doing it. I could go on and on about Dominick. He was my big brother and I really loved him.

I know that God loves him a whole bunch because he gave him this beautiful lady named Mary who was an angel walking on earth. She was perfect for Dominick; he had somewhat of a temper and she was calm. He loved to eat and she was the best of cooks. He was a perfectionist and she was as neat as a pin. They had two beautiful daughters, Rose Ann and DeDe. DeDe was a survival from a set of twins that Mary gave birth to during World War II. No matter what time of the day or night when we went to Dominick and Mary's home we were always offered something to eat, and I mean good, choice food. Her home was open to our entire family every Sunday afternoon. The fact is we all got together as a family at my mom and dad's home every Sunday afternoon. I mean the entire group and my dear mom fed all of us. When my mom and dad passed on, the gang went to Dominick and Mary's home. These are the kind of things that we don't see too much of in our high-tech world. As I share with you my memories of my family, my thoughts and my heart go back to the good old days when love was the biggest part of our lives.

Then there was my brother Art and his wife Florence, whom we called Flossie. My mother used to call him "Dolly" because when he came home from the Army she had not seen him for a long time and when she saw him she said, "Oh, my dolly is home!" So we brothers thought that was a cute name for him. So we often called him Dolly and the name kind of stuck with him through the years. I must admit he was truly a handsome guy with black curly hair and blue eyes. A personality second to none, with a decent singing voice. He played the saxophone and the guy got along with just about every human being on this earth. He was a carpenter by trade and ran many big construction jobs, building many homes throughout Southern California during his many years as a carpenter and foreman with a very large construction group that he worked for. Art's wife Florence was more or less the quiet type but she had a great interest in sewing, belly dancing and in general she attended many craft and educational classes offered by various schools and park districts. At this writing she is still with us and her five children see that she is well taken care of. One of their children, Michael, has been with the shoe giant, Nike, from day one. He was quite a runner in high school and received all kinds of awards and Nike spotted his success and asked him to come on board and join the company. He has been with them now for over 20 years. The next child in line was Dean. Dean was very successful in the business world and is also musically inclined, plays guitar and sings. I probably don't have the children in the right order; I think it is Donna who is second. She has many talents, she is a very pretty girl and she also had a bout with breast cancer. She is a survivor and now she's a volunteer for the cancer society and does much good work for them, bless her. Then along came Gino. He is kind of a quiet guy also. He is a paleontologist and works with the state. Whenever they do any digging for new construction work he gets in there and finds out if there are any archaeology items in the ground. To this day he has uncovered many, I don't know what you call them, but some of them were hundreds and thousands of years old. Gino is married to a very lovely lady named Lan from Vietnam. He met her in Vietnam and he brought her to America and they have three beautiful children. The last one to come along in Art's family was Lisa. She is also married to a great guy who goes by the name of Enrique. He is involved in the real estate and financial world.

My brother, Art, and I were the last to get married in the family. We had a great time together, we dated together, we did a lot of singing together. We both loved music, stayed on top of the latest records being released. We sat around and drank beer, during those fun years. Art was the kind of guy who could make something out of nothing. He would love to make long tapes of music of the big bands. He was a great gardener, great dad, loved playing cards and a great cook. I might add he did all the cooking for his entire family for many, many years. What stands out in my mind about my family, and is the main reason I decided to write this book, is the beautiful relationship that existed between Mom and Dad and all the family and all of the in-laws and people in general. I thank God and I praise him for all that he did for us.

I must tell you about this crazy little episode that occurred between my brothers and me one night. We occasionally went to see the Los Angeles Angels of the Pacific Coast League. It was AAA ball and at that time the Angels were owned by the Cubs. So we went to see a game and on the way home we decided to stop at a bar not far from home for a cold beer (another one). We all had Angel baseball caps on our heads. The bartender came to our table and took our order and at the time our conversations led him to believe that we were members of the Angel team. So he proceeded to ask us what position we played. He went around the table asking each of us. Art said second base, brother Al said left field, I said shortstop. When he got to my brother Dominick, who had not been listening to the entire conversation, so when he asked what do you play, he blurted out "guitar" and started strumming and loudly saying, "I play guitar." We laughed all the way home, life can be funny.

I would like to share with you the eulogy I wrote for my brother Art:

Dearest Brother Art,

I find that as I age, there are many thoughts of the past that come to mind and a majority of the time they come to me with the people who were closest to me. Mostly family members and some friends that were with me through life's hills and valleys.

I know that I had mentioned this to you in my last letter. I mean about the wonderful parents we had and how much fun and love we shared with them and between us brothers and sisters.

One thing too, Curly, that I am happy about is this. We were born during a great period of time. We weathered the Great Depression and we saw battle in World War II and had loads of fun after the war, when all of us in America made up for lost time.

As I look back on our lives, I am once again delighted that our parents were able to give us the love, the care, the concern and the discipline and probably in that order. It was absolutely amazing to me how well we lived. We had nourishing food, decent clothes, a clean home, an orderly home and plenty of love and respect. Let's face it, we had what it takes to call a house a home.

Sure there were times when we had to put cardboard in our shoes because of the holes in them and we used white string for shoe laces and had to get up a 5 a.m. to sell papers before we went to school. That gave us staying power, character, responsibility and a sense of accomplishment.

We passed our idle time away sitting in front of our home trying to name the cars, year and model as they went by and as we got older we used to try to stump each other on song titles and questions about band leaders, theme songs and best-selling records.

I am writing about places, persons and events as they come to mind, so it will appear that I am all over the boards, and I am.

I remember the time you and I went on a roller skating date with two girls. We had loads of fun but we would have been on our feet more, if we hadn't drunk a little too much port wine before we went skating. I haven't had port wine since.

I also remember when I was young, probably 5 or 6 years of age, I used to say to you, "make me laugh," and you used to do all sorts of funny things.

I remember one time you were reading to me and came upon a word called Dundee and I couldn't stop laughing. Why? I don't know. Maybe it was the faces you would make when you read to me.

After World War II, when we four brothers first got together after so many years, we had a party that lasted for a couple of days. I remember I had a terrible time getting time off from my job.

We four brothers entertained a lot of our relatives and friends, when we would go serenading at all hours of the night and early morning. We did a lot of this during the holiday season and in the off season as well.

I'll never forget when you were drafted in the Army in 1941. The war had not yet started and we were all at the age of fun. You with your saxophone, Al with his accordion, Busse with his guitar and me with my drums, and vocalizing.

Your going in the Army was quite a blow to all of us, but mostly to Ma and me. I recall the Sunday night before you left, that would have been March 2, 1941. I was so depressed because of your departure, I got up out of bed and went for a walk; it was after midnight. It was a lonely night for me, but thank God the war finally ended and we all had a great many fun-filled years.

I learned a lot from you, not about the produce business or my financial business but about life and people. Among the things I learned from you, I remember these things mostly:

How to:

Achieve personal accomplishments.

Make the best of what you have.

Make fun out of whatever you do.

Have patience when things get tough.

Make something out of nothing.

You have a great imagination. I was really proud of the way you took to the carpenter trade. You were so mechanically inclined in plumbing, electrical, cement work, cabinet making and finished carpenter work.

Gloria and I were so proud of that bookcase you made for us with the built-in radio and record player. It had musical notes mounted on the front of the cloth that cover the speakers. You had crafted them out of wood.

I guess one of the greatest things I admired about you was your patience. I recall the days I spent working with you when I left Safeway. You had a job on your hands trying to make a carpenter out of a produce man, but then expertise in dealing with people was one of your strongest suits.

I even cured my first batch of olives with your guidance.

I can see why Flossie, Mike, Donna, Dean, Gino and Lisa are all so fond and proud of you. You have the quality that people look for in a human being. Great guy, great father, great brother, great friend, great Uncle.

Then there are looks. All your female nieces, female cousins and girls in the neighborhood just loved your blue eyes and curly hair. I guess you were aware of that, I know I was. Girls never even looked my way when you were around. If they did speak to me it was to ask me where you were.

Even our mother used to call you, "MY DOLLY". I never heard her call me that, she did call me "Baboo" though and I know that is far away from Dolly.

As I come close to the ending of this time down memory lane, I can really say that I thank God for my folks, my brothers, sisters, nieces, nephews, all my relatives and friends, the work I have done, for the food I have consumed, for the clothes I wore, for the fun I have had and for the challenges I have had. It has been a good life.

We don't know what the future holds for us, but I wanted to share this with you while we are both still here on earth.

Curly, I remember on more than one occasion, I told Ma and Pa how happy I was to have been born of them.

Especially Ma for the real people matters, such as:

Self-love keeps us away from God.

Extending love to other people.

Self-knowledge, how we are related to God.

God is our only source of dependency, fulfillment and happiness.

Never lose faith in God or yourself.

Avoid anger, bitterness.

Accept challenges gracefully.

As a young man I remember Ma telling me this story about giving to others. She said, see the homes on our street? God sends the necessities of life to each home. As He does this, he says. I send things to each home, but I notice there are a couple of homes that send out goods from their home to others. But I never see anything coming from many of the other homes. I need to give the homes that are sharing more because they share theirs with others. That was from a woman who only went to the 4th grade in Italy.

Both you and I were blessed with beautiful wives and great children who love us, respect us and treat their fellow humans likewise.

Well, Curly, I wanted to share these thoughts with you. I know you share my sentiments about all that I talked about.

Thanks again, I am happy to have you as my brother and thanks for the many insights you gave me through the years, especially on humor, endurance, respect and love.

God bless you and yours in all that you do, think and say.

You leave us with a void in our hearts but you also left us a lot of memories of your goodness to fill that void. By imitating your ways, you will forever be with us.

As you read on in this book you will undoubtedly read more about some of my family members and some of my experiences that we had together.

My sister Teresa, I would have to compare with my sister-in-law Mary, they were both similar in character. Excellent wives, good mothers, good housekeepers, beautiful ladies. She married a gentleman by the name of Gregory. Greg as we called him was a genuine entrepreneur. If there was a deal that could be made of some kind you can bet that Greg would be there. There weren't too many areas that he didn't get involved with. Car sales and an excellent rate automotive mechanic, you name it, Greg sooner or later would be involved in it. My sister Teresa had three children, Mary Ann, Rosalie and as we called him, "Little Greg". Each one of them found a place in the world of professionals and all did very well for themselves and others.

I keep a photo of my sister Teresa's wedding day picture. The reason I keep the picture in my office is because she actually looks like an angel and her actions, her behavior, her thoughts, her feelings, her words were like those of an angel. I know I have mentioned the word angel amongst many of our family members but then again it's one of the main reasons this book came about. Not a day goes by that I don't thank God for putting me in such a beautiful family. Teresa died at the young age of 51. She had many illnesses during her lifetime. Why such things happen to such nice people is hard for us to understand. God knows why and I am certain the day will come when we will have those answers. Nevertheless, as is the case with many of my deceased family members, I speak of them often. I think about them often, I try to do some of the same things they did and I tell folks I am about the luckiest guy in the world to have had the grace of God to have such beautiful, lovely people as my family.

Then there was my brother Al and his dear wife, Rose. You are about to read a beautiful story about a lovely couple. My brother Al was loaded with talent, lots of guts, some fears and was pretty positive about everything. As for Rose, his wife, here we go again. She was one of the girls I mentioned earlier in the beginning of this book that fell into the category of the kind of girl I was looking for to become my wife. If you recall, I wanted to marry a duplicate of her and I did. Al and Rose had six children, Jeanne, Rita, Rosie, Joni, Sam and Christine. What beautiful children they were. To see that family going to mass on Sunday was a picture of beauty.

My brother Al and I both worked in retail markets for many years, me as a produce man and him as a butcher. At times we worked in the same store. He later went into construction and when he passed away he was working for the state of California highway divisions. Rose was a beautiful mother who took care of her children and all the good things that make up a home.

I still recall the day when Al and Rose came to our home shedding tears because the doctor had diagnosed a limping foot as polio on Rose's right leg. It was the beginning of the end. It wasn't polio that Rose had, it was Lou Gehrig's disease. From that point on my brother Al and his children had a great change in their normal way of life. The story is sad in many ways and yet in its own way, the way it was handled by my brother Al and his children, it was beautiful. Rose had to be fed, she had to be changed, she was unable to even shoo a fly from her nose. Who handled most of this responsibility was our dear little Rita because her dad felt as though her follow-through would be more consistent. And there was the age factor, some were old enough to help, some had other obligations that had to be met but at any rate, they struggled through. Rose finally passed away in 1957 and Al was left with six children. Al and his six children were shining examples of what can be accomplished when love enters the scene. If ever there was a reason to be extremely proud of those who love, my brother Al and his six children would make the headlines.

Jeanne was the oldest and first, and she was beautiful. Wonderful personality, great student, did some teaching, shared much of her time in charity work. She was also highly artistic, on a scale from one to ten, I would give her a great big nine. Jeanne married an attorney named Robert Slatten and they had a very handsome boy whom they named Steve. Both Jeanne and Bob have left this world, may God grant them eternal rest. Steve is married, has a lovely family. It is my understanding he is involved with the political world. Al and Rose had a second child named Rita. She was a tiny thing, still is not very tall. I clearly remember playing with her when she was an infant in her little crib. She had curly hair and could pass for the new Shirley Temple. At this point I should bring up the fact that all of Al and Rose's children pursued their own careers and I might add they paid their own way and gave of themselves whatever it took to achieve the desired results. And in Rita's case she wound up as a reporter on the San Diego Tribune and when they sold out, she entered into court reporter profession and she's also a writer. As you can see Rita has plenty of talent.

Al and Rose's third child was also a girl named Rosie. Rosie was one-of-a-kind. She knew what she wanted and she went after it. Rosie was a kind of girl who mirrored our son, Peter. They both had a mind of their own and did what they wanted. They could do whatever it took to accomplish their desired results and the best part of their character was, they were successful at what they went after. Rosie was also very artistic and she was quite a writer also. She was an idealistic person and had a very talented mind. She could envision so many things that she would like to do and for the most part she saw them through. One thing I notice about Rosie was she knew there were lines in life that were meant to be crossed, and cross them, she did. She met a black man by the name of Dwight Phillips, whom she thought had a lot going on and he did. The result of that marriage was three beautiful children. The children were named Misty, Dwight and Michael. And yes, there are grandchildren. I'm sorry to say I don't recall the exact count. As for Misty, I think I could write a book about her. She's beautiful, half Italian and half Afro-American but here's the best part. She is 100% beautiful human being. As for Dwight and Michael they are both doing great. I do not get to see them very often, so that's that. Not much for me to say about them.

Then we come to the fourth child in Al and Rose's beautiful family. Her name is Joni, she is the one I mentioned earlier in the book who was my inspiration to put all my words on paper about my life, my family and friends, etc. If I live long enough I would love to write a book about Joni. She is married to a doctor by the name of Sam Halpern. Dr. Sam specializes in cancer. I believe he also carries the title of Professor and lectures to cancer groups throughout the world.

Sam and Joni have four boys, Danny, Evan, Justin and last but not least Jose (their adopted son). I said I could write a book on Joni and I probably could without a problem. Joni, like most of the Calvano family, is a loving, compassionate and humble human being. Upon finishing her schooling, she became a writer and was not satisfied with just being a writer, she decided to become an attorney. Lo and behold, she became an attorney. After she became an attorney, she decided there were many people in her area that were not being treated fairly. So what did she do? She started a group called Supportive Parents Information Network - SPIN. SPIN helped parents by showing them how to lead a better life in all the areas that affect your way of living. Joni did this for 14 years and got the program well underway, then she handed the reins over to others. Joni believes in her creator, she believes in people. She helps people who need help. It doesn't make any difference if they need a ride to the doctor, help with their taxes, you name it, Joni does it. I know this about Joni, St. Peter is not going to have to ask Joni, what did you do while you were down there because what she's been doing she did all of her life. We love you Joni, stay on your present course and keep God as your planet, as you have done in the past.

I will be sharing at various times throughout this book about my feelings, my intimate thoughts and memories about my dear brother Al and his lovely wife Rose and their six children. I will share with you the portion of their lives that will live forever. I will get back to how proud I am of Sam and Christine also. I know it will also grab you where you can feel it in your heart.

Al did a lot of church work in his spare time and met a woman who was a secretary to a priest at the local parish. She too had a family. Her husband passed away, she was left with two children. Her name was Rosemary. Rosemary and Al became friendly and the day came when they got married. It seemed to be a big, saving event for both of them. As the old saying goes, "things aren't always what they seem to be." Rosemary turned out to be an alcoholic and from that point on became a major problem.

I received a call one Saturday morning at my office that my brother Al was picking olives up in a tree and the branch broke and he fell to the ground and he was in a coma. My experience I had the next couple of months I shall not ever put on paper. I remember telling folks when I joined the Marine Corps, I went in as a boy and came out as a man. In this particular case I went in as a man thinking I had seen everything and came out as a man knowing that I still had a lot to see before my final days.

Before my brother Al passed away, he would constantly want me to promise him I would take care of his kids if something happened to him. I jokingly would say to him that he would be around longer than I would. Then finally one day he asked me again and insisted that I give him an answer. At that time I assured him I would take care of his children. To go on to detail as to how this was accomplished is also more than what I care to discuss at this time. It was through the court system, we won guardianship of the children and we made our move. I want to say here now that my wife Gloria and I were taking on some extra responsibility. We both felt that God had blessed us by asking us to do some of his work for him and you know what? Those children were a blessing to us and we learned a lot about life. Then there was the fact that Al and Rose had done such a beautiful job bringing them up to the point where we took over, they were beautiful people. Unfortunately for them, Jeanne and Rosie have passed away but the remaining children Sam, Rita, Joni and Christine are all doing so beautiful, so dependable, so talented, so successful. I know that their mom and dad look down on them and say to each other, "while we were lifted, we left a great bunch down there."

I conclude this chapter by saying that we should remember as we go through life: EVERY EXIT IS AN ENTRANCE SOMEWHERE ELSE.

Chapter 5
MY EARLY EMPLOYMENT

My early employment days consisted of normal type jobs that a youngster would do, such as selling newspapers, paper routes, mowing lawns, cleaning garages for folks, etc. I did all of these jobs and then some. For example, I sold papers from a newsstand from 5:00 a.m. until 8:00 a.m. I had to walk a mile to the newsstand, a mile back home and this was in all kinds of weather. I recall the winter of 1935 and 1936, the temperature in Chicago never went above 6 degrees during the day and the lowest was 35 degrees below zero. Yes, I sold papers that morning and many, many cold mornings. In addition to selling papers, whatever few pennies I made, I was asked to stop at the bakery store and buy day-old bread for three cents a loaf. Did I mention I had to walk another mile to school? During the cold spell I mentioned above, I still recall the headline in the Herald American newspaper, "Heat wave hit Chicago, six above zero."

During this cold spell of 1935 and part of 1936, we lived in a seven-room flat as they called them in those days. It was huge. Fact is, it was so huge that we had sliding doors that separated the kitchen, dining room, living room and bedrooms. What I am about to tell you may sound like a fable. It got so cold at night in the bedroom portion of the house, we were forced to close the sliding doors and sleep

on the floor on our mattresses in the living room.
Being normal boys, we decided to see how cold it
actually got in the unheated portion of the flat. We
set a glass of water in that section and there was a
mad rush in the morning to see what happened to
the water. Guess what? It was frozen. Yes, indeed,
frozen solid. Believe it or not. Ripley is no longer
around, but what I'm telling you is the exact thing
that happened.

I also sold Sunday papers in our local Catholic
church, St. Joachim. Each Sunday there was a mass
every hour from 6:00 a.m. until noon. We sold the
Chicago Tribune at every mass.

Then there was what we called "junking". We
would walk up and down the alleys in our
neighborhood looking for brass, copper, foil, zinc,
lead, newspapers, which in turn we would sell to
the junkman when he came along.

As I mentioned earlier this was during the Great
Depression and things were really tough financially
speaking. My mom and dad had many dear friends
who would try to help us in different ways. I recall
a lady by the name of Rose and her husband Sam
who knew the manager of the Edison power plant
not far from our home. The Edison power plant
produced power with coal and they would have a
coal car alongside their plant periodically. They
would shovel it from the car via a shoot into their
building. In doing so there was always the
occasional piece or two or three, sometimes more,
pieces of coal that would fall on the ground. We
were allowed to gather any coal that fell on the
ground, place it in a burlap sack and take it home

for our use. Sometimes the coal car would sit for five or six days before it was completely unloaded and every day after school we would be there to pick up the pieces of coal; that was before we did our homework. We didn't mind, it was just a way of life, it was honest and it served us well too.

One of the summer jobs I recall was selling produce with Uncle Alex from his truck. He would buy straight loads of corn, straight loads of cantaloupes and watermelons and my brother Al and I would go knocking on doors with a basket of corn or cantaloupes or whatever we were selling. Some of the apartment buildings were four stories high and if you sold out your basket of produce and you were on the second floor that meant going back down to the truck and filling your basket up again. My brother received a dollar a week and I received .50 cents a week. That was for six days work, Monday through Saturday. One day I got brave enough to ask Uncle Alex why he paid my brother Al a dollar a week and me .50 cents a week and his answer was, "Because he's two years older." And I thought to myself what a horrible way to establish a wage rate, but again we needed the money and I wasn't about to quit the job.

This next experience I think made such a great influence on me that I really believe it is what got me interested in the produce business. My brother Al and I sat down one day and discussed the idea of buying produce at the State St. market and establishing our own little route to sell the produce. The first thing we needed was a vehicle. Our dad was a big help to us; he built us an oversized body of a coaster wagon. It was well made with sturdy high sides on it. My brother Al painted the slogan on the side, "Calvano Brothers Fresh Produce." Our motto - Quality Higher Than Price. The next thing we needed was working capital, and we were able to scrape up three dollars with the junk selling program and away we went.

The State Street market was at least three 3 miles from our home. We would take turns pulling the wagon one block for each of us then we would switch. Going to the market wasn't bad because the wagon was empty, but on the way back to the proposed route, it was a different story.

We had some experience with produce but the question was what can we buy that will hold up fairly well in an open wagon exposed to outside temperatures all day. So we tried various commodities like cucumbers, tomatoes, potatoes and green beans and occasionally we got some corn or maybe cabbage and when we had something of a more perishable nature we would wet burlap bags and place them over the product. Things went well for us, and there were many days when we sold out and there were many days when we had produce left over and we would take it home and it would be well taken care of by our dear mother. The one lesson I learned was the first day that we experienced very poor sales and practically all the produce was left on the wagon and that meant we didn't have our three dollar capital to buy produce for the next day's business. So I got the bright idea, let's reduce the price, get what we can out of it and that's what we did. I think we wound up with something like a $1 .75 so the next day we went to the market and bought a $1.75 worth of produce which kept us alive. From that day on we were more alert to our pricing structure, more alert as to when to reduce prices and alert to purchase items that could hold overnight. We were quite proud of our first business venture. We enjoyed a profitable summer. I might add in those days when we earned any money, it was wrong to keep it, so it went to our dearly beloved mother who could stretch a dime into a dollar when it came to feeding the family.

I also remember when one of our sisters got married, it was out of town, North Judson, Indiana. My brother Al and I were not able to attend because we could not afford to miss our newspaper job selling papers on Saturday and Sunday. But we were rewarded with goodies that were brought back to us in form of wedding cake, candy and etc. All for the good old days.

Thinking back to those days, sometimes things seemed kind of hard. But the love, the warmth, the care, and the concern we received from our parents made it all worthwhile. They had been sort of tough on us but it was no picnic for them either. I recall reading Tom Brokaw's book on the Greatest Generation and I remember to tell our dear Lord thank you for giving me the opportunity to be born in that generation.

I conclude this chapter on my early employment with this comment. Dealing with the public in the business world is a great way to achieve knowledge of people in general. It is also a great way to increase your decision-making ability.

Chapter 6
DO UNTO OTHERS
AS THOUGH YOU WERE THE OTHERS

In this chapter I will share my efforts to live my life as the title of this chapter suggests. Was I always successful in achieving that goal? No, I was not. Why did I not achieve my desired goal? Did I know the reason why?

Yes, I did. It was because I broke away from the 10 commandments. Please allow me to say in advance, this chapter is not about my religion or any religion for that matter. Rather it's about doing things a certain way, because it is the right way to do them.

The religious devotions I will share with you are devotions I felt that I needed to do things the right way.

I was born and raised a Catholic. I did not attend Catholic school but we did practice our religion. I might add we practice it as best we can and I am certain we slipped and fell occasionally. My mom and dad, especially my mom, graciously did her best to keep us on track. I still remember when she would talk about some future trip, picnic, etc. She would say, "The good Lord willing." So I would say I had a good foundation about trying to live the 10 Commandments. For the most part we attended church every Sunday and as I mentioned earlier, we sold Sunday papers at masses on Sunday so we would catch the first mass at 6 A.M.

Before I proceed further, I will say that at an early age I rationalized in my own mind that I was a much better human being when I included God in my life daily, as opposed to forgetting about God completely or perhaps being with God on a part time basis. Very basic and very elementary, but it just made sense to me. Why? That's the way it works for me.

Christmas Eve was a great holiday. It was all in preparation for the coming of baby Jesus. Our Christmas Eve dinner table was a sight to behold. Twenty-one different dishes. To mention just a few of the items, there were codfish, fried smelts, broccoli with shrimp, Italian fried bread, homemade noodles, spaghetti sauce made with shrimp or squid, chestnuts, all varieties of fruits, candy of all sorts, homemade bread, homemade dago red, home cured olives with mushrooms and so many other items. We would generally be up until midnight. My mother always made it a point to leave all the nonperishable dishes on the table that night in honor of the Bambino (baby Jesus). Talk about love and good food and good people, we were blessed by God.

There were two busy periods in our Italian neighborhood, as I shall briefly describe, that really were something the whole neighborhood waited for. Each year after Rosary Sunday, which is usually after the first Sunday in October, four to six families would get together and buy a truckload of zinfandel wine grapes. A truckload is usually about 600 lugs of grapes. We usually split them up between the families and during that same period, each family would slaughter a pig. From the grapes came the good old "dago red". The fall selling season that I mentioned earlier gave us the peppers, tomatoes, eggplant, green beans and green tomatoes and boy did they taste good and come in handy during the wintertime. We had a huge winepress that would hold about 25 lugs of grapes. It had a big long handle and it took four men to walk and turn it, to squeeze the grapes. As this was going on they were taking sips of the wine that they made the previous year and eating Italian sausage that they had made from the previous years' slaughtered pig. This usually went on until about 2:00 or 3:00 in the morning, or until the job was completed. So in summary, we had plenty of canned tomatoes, canned tomato sauce, canned bell peppers with mushrooms with a tomato flavor, salted eggplant, canned green beans, Italian sausage cured in quart containers and olive oil and a good glass of wine to wash it all down. So you see we had fun making all these things and we really had a jolly good time consuming them.

There is one other area that probably most folks would not even attempt today. The brother-in-law that I spoke of, with the ricotta factory also lived on a farm that had 180 acres, and about 40 acres of the 180 acres was a wooded area with lots of trees and leaves on the ground and that made an ideal growing area for mushrooms. We would walk through the woods at the proper time, usually in late fall. It was so exciting to hit an area where you see the ground cracked from mushrooms coming up. I do remember us bringing back home sometimes 10 to 15 burlap bags full of mushrooms. It took us hours to clean them, then later we had to salt them and put them in quart jars, sautéed of course. We also put them up in jars with oil, vinegar and garlic and later added them to our spaghetti sauce for future meals.

As most of us know, Italy produces many olives. Amongst the Italian people, home cured olives fall into the category of homemade wine, homemade sausage, wild mushrooms and several other food items that the Italian people preserve.

Come the month of November olives are ready to be picked. It is then that you will see the Italian people climbing olive trees, shaking the branches and gathering the green and black olives to take home for curing. The curing process is slow and tedious. For example - green olives. First of all they have to be graded for quality, second, each individual olive has to be gently tapped with a hammer. This forces you to wear gloves during this procedure or your fingers will be badly stained. Once they are all tapped and split, they are then placed in pillowcases and the pillowcases full of olives are tied at the end and placed in a crock of water. That water is changed every day for approximately 4 to 6 weeks. You must be careful of the area where the water is poured; nothing will grow in that area for many years. When the olives have lost their bitter taste, you then remove them from the pillowcase and place them in ceramic crocks and season them with salt, hot red pepper, olive oil, oregano, fennel seed, etc. Then place a wooden lid, be certain that it fits in the inside diameter of the crock. Then, put a heavy weight on top of the wooden lid and allow them to cure for whatever time it takes. When you have reached the desirable taste, place into quart jars and add additional seasoning, if you desire and you might want to add some of those wild mushrooms that you picked and sautéed. Now when you eat them all you need is some of my mother's homemade bread and some of my dad's homemade wine. Excuse me, I think I'll stop for a moment and have some of my olives and mushrooms with a little bit of homemade bread and a good glass of wine.

Later in life I got more involved in church activity. While I was in the Marine Corps I became closely united with priests of our division. I have inserted a picture of what the Marines built for midnight mass on the island of Pelilieu. It was an old flatbed trailer filled with Palm fronds, with a small step-up area for the choir of eight Marines. Tomato cans, number 10 size, filled with sand to hold the Palm fronds in place. All in all, as you can see, it served the purpose well.

As you can well understand, at the age of 92, I have had to put on my thinking cap. Over the past few months I've racked my memory about this exciting life I have led over the past umpteen years. I recall shortly after I was released from the Marine Corps my brother Al and I (May he rest in peace) did some odd jobs together. So we got the bright idea to run a little add in the local paper advising folks that we do odd jobs like cement work, cleaning yards, trimming trees, pulling weeds, minor carpenter work, etc. We did quite well and my dear brother suggested that each day after work we would go home and kneel before the statue of Jesus and thank him for the labor and the income for the day.

Another thought that came to mind as I research my old brain was this. On our wedding night my darling wife and I were members of a Catholic group called "night adoration in the home". The devotion consisted of one hour of prayer from 3:00 A.M. to 4:00 A.M. once a month. It just so happened that on our honeymoon night was our turn for night adoration. So on our first night together we spent one hour with Jesus from 3:00 – 4:00 A.M. We thought that was a beautiful way to begin our married life. We are now on year 66 and we still have night adoration from 3:00-4:00 once a month.

For the past 20 years I've been very active in my parish functions and been involved with practically every ministry in the parish. Some of my functions consisted of Parish Council President, building committee member, Eucharistic minister. For 10 years I was leader of the Stephen ministry program which is a non-denominational ministry group that assists those with life's problems. I attended training for the leadership of this program at Marymount College in Los Angeles and it proved to be a very beneficial program to many. It involved a 26-week course and during those 26 weeks we dealt with those who have problems with divorce, hospitalization, suicide, job loss, bereavement, depression. We helped out many folks during the 10 years that the ministry was in operation.

I am currently a Eucharistic minister at the local hospital and visit from 40 to 60 patients each Tuesday. My visits consist of offering Holy Communion, praying together, listening and offering words of encouragement. I'm now nearing my 11th year in the program.

I also visit those who are homebound, folks at rest homes and I do a pretty large amount of phone work keeping in touch with people who are recuperating and bedridden. I have one patient that I have visited for the last 12 years that I visit 2 to 3 times a week. I offer him communion, read to him or just sit and listen to him.

That pretty much takes care of my activity with me and my church work over quite a few years. Hopefully, God will still give me a desire, the ambition and the grace to continue helping those in need until I check out. Here's something I'd like to share with you. Helping people really and truly helps the caregiver just as much, if not more than the care receiver.

To you the reader, please accept my explanation of my version of church and religion in this chapter.

It is not my intention to show favoritism to any one religion. It wasn't my intention to preach religion to those who read this book. As I said in the beginning of this book titles, SUCCESS COMES IN CANS - FAILURE COMES IN CAN'TS. The experiences, incidents, religious practices or any subject matter presented to you in this chapter are things that I have experienced that are my beliefs. I am merely sharing my life experiences with each of you. Please accept the contents of this chapter as ways, means, beliefs and locations that occurred during my life time. This is what I did, I said, and I believed. It is all mine and, last but not least, boasting is out of the question, these are merely the facts of my life.

To summarize this chapter, my mom and dad displayed to us children their love for Jesus, by example. They gave love and accepted that love, they were joyful and had good times, and were patient in times of trial and suffering. My parents also told me that we would never know how happy a person could be until we gave of ourselves to others, and boy, these are words that I shall never forget. You might call this the frosting on the cake. There are two occasions in life that will really make you feel like you're on top of the world. I list them here for you: 1. You will never enjoy such great happiness than when you forgive a person who has harmed you. 2. You will never enjoy such great happiness as when you are forgiven by a person you have harmed.

Trust me, it's a grand and glorious feeling.

During my lifetime I have experienced living with God full-time, living with God on a part-time basis and living without God. By far, living with God on a full time basis has proven to be the right choice for me. My greatest desire is to follow the teachings of Jesus that I have received in reading and digesting his many parables. In simple layman language, in reading his parables this is where the inspiration came in. How can you not believe the teaching of Jesus after reading His Parables?

For example, *let he who is without sin cast the first stone, render unto Caesar the things that belong to Caesar, the first shall be last and the last shall be first, he who will exalt himself will be humbled, he who humbles himself will be exalted, he gave from his surplus, she gave from her needs, no one can be a slave of two masters. He will love one and hate the other or he will be loyal to one and despise the other.* As you well know there are many, many more parables. If you believe that Jesus was not the son of God, He was a great man with the answers to life.

Jesus promised us, *I am, I will always be with you, I love you, trust me.*

I gave my heart to Jesus because he gave up his life for me. Jesus gives me the kind of peace that the world cannot give me. This makes my yoke easy, and my burden light. He helped me to bring to others generosity, kindness, forgiveness, patience, love, and obedience, which is my way of bringing Jesus to others.

Chapter 7
MY MILITARY SERVICE TIME

War is hell. It definitely has a way of disrupting the lives of every human being. As I mentioned earlier, my brothers and I had a little band which included the following instruments, guitar, accordion, saxophone and drums. We had a lot of fun playing at parties, weddings and just horsing around in our basement.

Along came World War II and on March 3, 1941, our brother Art was one of the first to be drafted. The breakup was hard on all of us. Not only did it break up our band but also our lovely brotherhood relationship. I recall one thing very vividly, on the night of March 2, I couldn't sleep thinking about my brother leaving us and going off to war. It was about midnight so I got fully dressed, took a walk around the block. As it turned out, I went around the block many times. It was my way of handling his departure.

Before the war ended my mom and dad proudly gave up their sons to the U.S. military. Three in the Army and one in the Marine Corps. As I said earlier, war causes problems in many areas. My mother was really heartbroken when my brother Art went into the service. The U.S. had not yet declared war and my brother Art was stationed in California, so my mom decided to take a trip to California, since we had relatives who lived close to where my brother

Art was stationed. Upon her return from his visit she fell in love with California. She said it was so much like Italy, she would move out there. So as time went on we discussed it as a family and decided we would make the move. First ones to move there would be my mom and dad and my brother Al and I. Lo and behold immigration department stated for my mother that aliens were not allowed to travel. My mom had not as yet become a citizen, so my brother Al and I immediately wrote a letter to the American consulate in Los Angeles. The letter was informative, polite and included one big factor. Why couldn't my mother move to California when she was going to have four sons in the U.S. military very soon? They were cooperative and replied back saying that permission was granted. My mom became a citizen shortly after arrival in California.

I was next in line to enter the service so I got the bright idea to enlist in the Marine Corps. There was one small catch to it; I was only 18 years of age. In those days, to volunteer on your own you had to be 21. It took me three months to convince my mom to sign my enlistment papers, and I might add, she did it with tears in her eyes. So I was off to the Marine Corps.

I remember very clearly the first statement that came out of our boot camp sergeant's mouth: "I want all you guys to remember one thing, when the going gets rough and things aren't like they used to be at home, remember one thing, we didn't ask for you, you volunteered." I thought to myself, what a warm and friendly greeting.

I must say one thing for the Marine Corps; I went in a boy and came out a man. The boot camp training in those days wasn't easy and you didn't dare complain in letters to people back home about any particular situation because our mail was censored.

Before I got out of boot camp I thought my name was Calvano U. Shitbird, Calvano was my first name, U was my middle initial and my last name was SHITBIRD.

I recall several incidents that occurred in boot camp between boot camp trainees and the drill sergeants. We were out in the field in the shade of a tent going through the nomenclature of the M1 rifle. There happened to be a stray dog close to the tent and one of the Marine trainees was being rather friendly to it. So the sergeant called him up in front of the whole group and in a very serious matter said to him, "Do you like dogs?" His answer was, "Yes." "You have a dog at home?" His answer was, "Yes." "You know a lot about dogs?" His answer was, "Yes, quite a bit." "Well, then you get down on all fours and walk like a dog, bark like a dog, raise your leg and pee like a dog and sit up like a dog." To make a long story short, it was embarrassing. To top things off, the drill sergeant informed us to stop that laughing, that this wasn't funny. We were here to learn about the M1 rifle not how to care for dogs.

Then there was the trainee who called his rifle a gun. The drill sergeant called him up front and told him to take his penis out, hold it in his right hand and his M1 rifle in his left hand and say very clearly, "This is my rifle, this is my gun," and to repeat 50 times with no laughing.

Then there was the trainee who dropped his rifle on the ground. That night he had to sleep with everybody's rifle in his bunk and the drill Sergeant said, "Don't let one of those rifles fall off that bunk tonight." I do not recall the number of rifles he had to sleep with but he didn't get any sleep.

Before shipping out for overseas we were in our barracks for further training on firearms etc. What I am about to tell you now is probably the funniest thing I've heard of, because it was as though it was a planned affair. There was a Marine who played in the band and this one particular night he came in late and some of the Marines decided to fill a rubber with water and place it under his blanket because he came in after lights out. And so when he sat on his bunk the rubber broke and there went water all over his bunk. He went to get the Sergeant. The Sergeant turned the barracks light on, stated that if the persons responsible for this don't come forward the whole barracks would be restricted from liberty for 30 days. When he completed his statement he turned the lights out and after he did, a Marine yelled out, "Give me liberty or give me death." The Sergeant immediately yelled back, "Who said that?" The Marine yelled back, "Patrick Henry, stupid."

Finally the big day came, the border troopship joined the convoy at the New Hebrides Islands and from there we headed for Peliliu Island. As stated, war is hell, and casualties were many. Loss of life was horrendous. One thing that most disturbed me was to see other Marines trying to remove teeth from dead Japanese soldiers, but then we humans see things differently.

I shall attempt to give you my understanding as to why we invaded the Palau Islands. The Palau Islands are a group of islands located approximately 500 miles from the Philippines. They are part of the Caroline Island group. Capturing Peliliu Island, an island in the Palau group, would enable us to establish an airbase, thereby neutralizing the entire Palau Island group, including Babeldaob, which contained 40,000 Japanese soldiers. At the same time it would be another stepping stone toward the road to the Philippines. Our planes flew constant flights to Babeldaob on bombing missions, using explosive bombs and napalm bombs.

The Japanese made a couple of attempts to send troops to Peleliu from Babeldaob but they were dead in the water, or so goes the story. Peleliu was to be captured in 72 hours but it actually took 71 days. Then we learned after the war that the Palau group could have been bypassed completely. I was not a part of the initial landing but we suffered casualties. A round from an army mortar shell fell behind us and fell short. I tried to remove as much from my memory as possible.

I served a little over three years in the Marine Corps and I must say it was quite an experience. It did me a world of good in more ways than I can explain at this time.

I made it to corporal. I don't recall what our pay was at that time but whatever it was I didn't use any, as there really was no need for the monthly money. I sent it to my mother and when I got home she had saved enough money for me to buy my first car. It was a 1937 Coupe. God bless my mom, may she rest in peace. She was really a very special lady in more ways than one and to many, many people.

When I got out of the Marine Corps my brothers and my dad had bought an empty lot and were building a house and they decided that I should be the breadwinner, so I went to work for a national food store chain, 11 days after getting home.

Those who have experienced combat are affected by it in many different ways. There are those who refuse to talk about it. There are those who block it out from their minds completely. There are those who remember certain incidents constantly. There are those who become active in any group whether it be a political group or a community group who oppose war.

I had a brother who upon returning from the war refused ever to go to a church service, even to the point of refusing to be best man at my wedding.

I chose not to discuss CLB parts of war and rather concentrate on what it did for me as a human being. It made me realize more than ever that wars come about when human beings turn their backs on God and try to force their way of life on other humans. I place my faith in God and times of peace, war or good times, bad times with goods folks, not so good folks, etc.

This is why I made this my philosophy, I don't have to like you or your way of life and you don't have to like me or my way of life. We owe it to each other to treat each other with dignity because we were both created by God. In conclusion, the teeth of that Japanese soldier still belong to him. War is hell and people are people. We are obligated to defend our human body and our home and our families to the best of our ability. In the end when we are called upon to do this, that's the time we have to say, "Let go and let God."

That about concludes my service time. There is much more that I could go into detail about, but I would rather not. To close on a happier note, I was so overjoyed and proud the way the people of the United States responded to the call during World War II, both on the military side and on the civilian side. Tom Brokaw in his book the Greatest Generation, named that generation correctly.

I would now like to share this letter written on April 20, 1942, by my dear mother. It was written to her sons who had enlisted in the service. It also was translated by my sister-in-law, Mary.

chicago 20 aprile 1942

Miei Carissimi figli

Oggi appunto o ricevuto la vostra cara lettera sono assai contenta che stote bene, e che siete arrivati sani e salvi solo che avete sofferto di fame e di stanchi; io lo sapeva che non avevate bastante per mangiare, ma se voi non bevarate troppo e stavate a casa insieme con me almeno l'ultimo giorno che dovevate partire io vi preparava un po' di tutto, ma voi di me ne avete fatto poco conto come sarei stata la vostra schiava non o potuto avere l'onore una Domenica di vedervi serii e mangiare uniti ma mi avete lasciato sola, e dopo che poi mi vedete morta allora penzate cosa vuol dire madre mia fermi e troppo dardi, io ora era il tempo che mi poteva stare un po' tranquilla che vi avia cresciuto che dopo

chi è maritato e chi soldato io non
vi posso avere a mio desiderio era bastan
te la pena di attilio, che si trova
sotto il comando delle armi e non ne
sono padrona e non so' dove me lo
mandono ci volevate anche voi che di
chi siete partito la notte non posso
mai dormire, perche sopra di tante
disturbi, e pure mi viene più dipenza
se attilio ora che ci manchate voi ma
voi lo so' che non ve ne incaricate
per nessuna cosa sicche' me la
debo prendere come Iddio me la
manda e quando muoro si pianta
la croce, e segno che questo deve
essere il mio destino, sono contenta
che vi piace a California, e vi auguro
buona fortuna, io lo so che vi piace,
pure a me mi piacera, ma non ci
o patuto venire, ora mio voglio stare
se qui la cosa voi sapete che lavoro
già trovato e devo muovere la prima
di magio quando non posso paghara
tisico la lista e me ne vado, dopora

ai quelra ccuura cre avraum ....
a Los Angeles, non ebbi nessuna
risposta e segno che non ci anno fatto
nessuno impegno, sicché mi devo mettere
con la mia testa a posto, e non se ne
parla più perché oggi o pagato $42,5c
per il mio appartamento, e ora lo so
come me lo passo, il meglie meglie
giornate a piangere, che oggi o ricevuto
pure la lettera di attilio e mi dice pure
tante di te che e stato contento che vi
siete veduti e stato assai sorpreso a
vederoi però mi dice che lo mandano
fuori della california, ma non mi
dice dove lo mandono, e dice che mi
fà una cartolina prima che arriva
sicché, io non o voglia di andare a
nessuna parte più se prima non
vedo cosa fà lui, la mia speranza
era che lo lasciovono a California ma
ora, sono come una perduta e non
so cosa penzare, non mi credevo
che lo mandavono lontano e voi
due essere pure fuori di casa

adesso non mi manca niente
che mi passo le giornate proprio
come le voglio io. spero che presto
finisce questa guerra e presto verrà
la mia contentezza, sento che tutti
sono stati contenti a vedervi. Dunque
dici a Maria e a tutti gli altri che come
ora non cio testa di scrivere se prima
non so dove si trova tuo fratello a che
posto lo fanno stare, scrivetemi subito
che io sto impenziero, e mi fate sapere
se vi a scritto attilio e se lo ...
più di che siete arrivati e fatemi
una carità di non bevere che sapete
che siete lontani di casa e io non
prendo riposo, che per il bevere troppo
vi siete castigati a partire di casa, basta
a avuto il telegramma e le cartoline voi
sapere se sono quieti senza di voi credo
che tu la penzi così, ma io però non
sono quieta che mi sento perduta tanti
baci di vostro padre e salutiamo a tutti e io
vi bacio coromente vostra mamma,
Rose Calva

TRANSLATION OF ROSE CALVANO'S LETTER

*Precisely today I received your dear letter. I am
very happy that all you are well and that you have
arrived healthy and unharmed, except for suffering
from hunger and fatigue. I knew it that you did not
have enough to eat but if you did not drink so
much and you were home together with me at least
the last day that you had to leave, I would have
prepared enough of everything. You would have
done little as I would have been your slave. I was
not able to have the honor of a woman to see you
eat together. Now I was left alone and after that I
saw death. Think what it means to a mother not to
be allowed to give so much to you, It was now the
time that I was alone after those who married and
those who became soldiers. It was not my wish to
have the pain of Attilio, that he was found under
the command of the army and I am not in control
and I do not know where they are sending him. I
begin the night but I cannot sleep, because I suffer
from so much disturbance. I worry mostly about
Attilio now that they are sending us you, but you
will not be responsible for anything. I must take
what God sends me and when he gives me a cross
to bear and a sign that this must be my fate, I am
content that you like it in California and I wish you
good luck. I know you want me to like it, but there
is no agreement to come now. I want to pursue
the thing you know I had already found and I have
to move the first of May when I am able to pay to
leave the list. And I am still anchored to that letter
that we wrote in Los Angeles, there was no answer
and sign that there was no one-year commitment
so I have had to put my head in place and no one
speaks more. That is why today I paid $42.50 for
my apartment. And now as I pass the better part*

of my days weeping, today I receive the letter of Attilio he tells me the same of you, that he is happy and very surprised to see you, but he tells me that they send him out of California but does not tell me where they send him, and I do not want to make a postcard until I know what he does. My hope is not to discover gold in California; I know I am lost and I don't know what to think. I can't believe they are sending him so far away and you two will be out of the house as well now. I don't want anything but to pass the day just as I am. I hope this war ends soon, and soon will be my happiness, I feel that all will be happy to see this, so say Maria and all the others, if this were written in gold, it would not suffice if first I do not know where your brother has been made to go. Write me right away so that I do not worry. If you have written Attilio or you have seen him more and you have been together, have the charity of not drinking too much when you are visiting so far from home. I do not take rest if something happens to you away from home. It would be enough if you sent a telegram or postcard. You know I am quiet when I don't hear from you, but I am nevertheless not calm and I feel lost. Many kisses from your father and good wishes from everyone. I kiss you sweetly.

Your mama,

Rose Calvano

Chapter 8
MY THOUGHTS ON MARRIAGE

I don't know at what age I began to notice girls. I was probably a little older than the average boy because I was so committed to responsibilities that were given to me by my parents. I'm not complaining because it was out of necessity that the responsibilities were given to me.

As I mentioned earlier, I wasn't very talkative as a youngster but I must say I was very observant. I was an excellent listener and had a photographic mind and for that matter I still do, even at my old age.

I think I inherited some of my mother's characteristics and my love for God helped me put the finishing touches on them. I guess listening was just part of my nature because even to this day I still do a lot of listening before I speak on a matter. Perhaps it was because I didn't want to make myself look like fool. I would participate in the conversation when I was well-versed on the subject matter.

Back to my thoughts on marriage. I knew the kind of girl that I wanted, one who would have the qualities I was looking for. I remember my mother telling me to eliminate a lot of problems in the marriage by marrying into your own nationality and your own religion. I am certain that this doesn't always work out the way we would like it to, but basically it's very elementary and it does make sense. My mother would always tell us to observe the way our intended spouse treats and respects their parents because that's pretty much what you can expect from her after your marriage. I found this to be true and an old saying tells us that we are a product of our environment.

I was born a Catholic and I believe in God. As Catholics we received the sacrament of baptism, first communion, confirmation and matrimony. These are the ones that I was concerned about until the time of my marriage. Mary, the mother of God showed us to pray the rosary. Without going into detail on how to pray rosary, let me just say, it's a special form of prayer and Mary, the mother of God, introduced it to St. Dominic in the 12th century. So I prayed the rosary frequently and still do to this day. I included it in my prayers asking God's help to serve faithfully each day of my life, to love others as I love myself, helping to find a nice woman to be my wife, and my prayer list was long. Long enough where it was necessary to write my prayer request down on what I called my prayer list and I still do that to this day. It's a matter of a way of life with me. I add a prayer request to my list as they appear and remove others as the prayers are answered.

Marriage to me is a big sacred, special event in life. When you stop and consider the two people are going to merge into one and going to have to agree on many things, whereas in the past each person made their own decisions as they saw fit. Perhaps the biggest event in being married is the fact that you and your spouse can pro-create. Stop and think, you're bringing additional people into the world and your philosophy, your training, your love, your discipline, your concern, your protection for what you and your spouse co-created becomes your responsibility.

That brings me to mind when I served as a Eucharistic minister at St. Mary's Hospital in the town where I live. When I got to the maternity ward I extended my usual greeting, then proceeded to tell the husband and wife, if they were both available, that it is wonderful having a baby. It's so exciting, it's like a miracle. It's not like a miracle, it is a miracle. It brings so much joy and happiness for both husband and wife. Along with happiness and the excitement comes a good share of your newborn babies' responsibility to both of you. What little Johnny or Mary eats, says, or wears, for that matter, just about everything that they do, is going to be your responsibility. I must say probably 99% of the couples that I delivered this message to accepted it with open arms and rightfully so.

My wife Gloria and I seldom went out to dinner when our kids were little, because we didn't want to disrupt the routine we had developed with the children. If we ever did go out to dinner there were only three babysitters that we approved. My mother-in-law, my two nieces, Rose Ann and DeDe, and my mom who could very seldom arise because of her health.

Each Sunday after church, people would stop us and say they had never seen four children behave like our children. How do you do it? We did it because we devoted our time, talent and attention to fulfilling their needs and requirements. And when we said no, it was not the wishy-washy "no" you hear so often nowadays. To this day we see the beautiful effects of the time and attention that we devoted to our children. It certainly is evident in their children. We have 13 grandchildren and 23 great-grandchildren and each one of them is just as evident with love, respect, responsibility, humor, dependability, all those good things that make life worthwhile.

It used to amaze me how when I worked in the produce department at the supermarket I would see mothers come in the store with a two- to three-year-old in the shopping cart and the mother politely asked the child what kind of vegetable she/he would like for dinner. I used to think to myself, like he's really intelligent that he knows the kind of food that is good for him at two or three years old. Like the saying goes, people will always be people.

Gloria and I are in our 66th year of marriage and we've had our differences of opinion, but with the God-given talents that we have, we sat down and worked them out. I recall reading a story about a couple that were married 79 years and when the husband was asked to what he attributed the success of his longtime marriage, his answer, always very simple, was: you give and take and compromise.

I could go on and on but I believe by this time you got the message that I was trying to deliver. Marriage can be beautiful but remember it takes two to tango.

What would I change in my marriage if I had it to do over again? Not a thing. I don't worry about things; I leave that up to God. I just tell Him my plans and rest assured that He will tell me if I'm headed the right direction or trying to take the shortcut.

I feel pretty much about marriage as I do about the time we were born in. I thank God for both of them. As the title to this book implies, SUCCESS COMES IN CANS, FAILURE COME IN CAN'TS.

I have learned from years of experience that using God as my pilot, and not as my co-pilot, helped me to head the right direction at the right time and in the right place.

In the Bible we read in Philippians, Chapter 4:13, "I can do all things through Jesus who gives me strength."

My wife Gloria and I have been married for 66 beautiful years. Out of those 66 years we have gone on early morning walks for about 25 of those years. Early morning for Gloria and me was 5:00 a.m., be it spring, fall or winter. During the standard time we carried a flashlight. It was our way of letting folks see us. As we walked we prayed the rosary. We praised God and thanked him for our parents, our family members, each other, our children, their children, our jobs, the money we earned, the food we consumed, the clothes we wore, for our friends, and yes, foes also, for our home and the list went on and on. Last but not least we praised God for giving up his life for the love of us.

Chapter 9
MY DEAREST FRIENDS

I have heard it said that a true friend is a person you could call at 2:00 A.M. when you had a problem and without any conversation that person would be at your side and at your beck and call. I think most of us would agree that the above pretty much describes the qualities of a true friend.

Let's step back a few steps and think about what prompted this person to become a true friend. What qualities did he or she possesses that made you feel you could call on this person any time of the day or night for help?

I would like to share with you some friends that I had who fit the criteria of a true friend over and over again during our relationship. The one ingredient that a true friend displays and in large fashion is the ability to give of themselves. As the late screen legend, Katherine Hepburn, once said, love has nothing to do with what you're expected to get, only with what you are expecting to give, which is everything.

I once met a gentleman by the name of Bob Wall. Bob loved people. He showed his love not by words but by deeds. Bob was a twin, he and his brother both served on aircraft carriers. During World War II Bob flew a F4U fighter aircraft and his brother was an anti-aircraft gunner on the Lexington.

Bob and I met through our church ministries and we became good friends. We attended mass together every day, served on several church ministries, helping those in need and occasionally we spent some time together downing a couple of beers and reminiscing about our younger days, our war days.

As we were driving in his car one day we came upon a handicapped person who was accepting donations from people passing by. Bob asked me if I thought we have time to give a donation before the light changed. I said probably not, it would be pretty close. Bob was determined. He said, "Gene, I just can't drive by that handicapped person without making some kind of a donation." We had gone about four or five blocks from where the gentleman was located and what does Bob do, he turns the car around, goes back to where the handicapped person was located, finds a parking spot and goes up to the gentleman and makes his donation.

One morning after mass we were engaged in a conversation about traveling, and out of the clear blue Bob says, "Gene, I would like to take you and Gloria to Italy." He continued to say I had helped him quite a bit in my financial picture and he would like to do that for me.

My reply to him was, "Bob, I could not accept your offer, and I know that Gloria will share my feelings also. Whatever I did for you doesn't warrant a trip to Italy. At any rate among friends we just help each other out when in need."

This went on for a couple weeks and finally Gloria and I both agreed that we should accept his offer. Needless to say we made the trip. We had a beautiful time seeing a good portion of Italy. We visited places like Rome, Naples, Padua, the catacombs, Pompeii, the isle of Capri, etc. It really and truly was a dream vacation.

Upon our return home, we continued with our beautiful relationship and our church involvement. Bob had gotten involved in a ministry that was helping those in need. In particular, those with personal and domestic problems. He said he was in kind of deep, and he would appreciate it if I could take over a portion of the leadership in the ministry.

Between the two of us we were able to get the ministry on a successful road. Shortly thereafter, Bob developed a heart condition and he had a feeling he would not be around long.

My daughter Annie and her husband had moved to Washington, DC. Ed was in charge of the Federal Prison Education System throughout the country. We had decided to take a trip and visit them.

Bob Wall said, "Gene, before you go, if something should happen to me while you're gone, I want to be sure that you are the one who does my eulogy." After several minutes of conversation, I promised Bob that I would do his eulogy if he passed on.

Well, when we got to DC, we unpacked and got settled in for a 10-day stay. The second day we were there the phone rang. It was Bob Walls's son, to say that his Dad had passed away. Just before he passed away he had told his son that if he didn't get through this he wanted his son to call me to come and do his eulogy and make certain that if this interrupted my vacation, to pay airfare for me to come home to do the eulogy and also to return back to Washington DC to continue my vacation.

That, dear friends, is a true friend. Bob taught me that being kind is more important than being right.

Mom and Dad have said to me on more than one occasion, and I'm sure they weren't the originators of this statement because I've heard it from other sources through the years: "If you can count the number of true friends that you have in your lifetime on one hand, you will have had what most people never receive."

During my lifetime I believe I can truthfully say I had two true friends. Oh yes, there were those who came awfully close to being true friends.

My second true friend was a gentleman by the name of Eddie Gendel. Eddie and his brothers owned a business in Los Angeles called the Los Angeles Nut House. Eddie told me that the way his dad started their business was under a rather unusual set of circumstances.

They were in the wholesale produce business and for some reason there were two carloads of peanuts, and for unknown reasons the railroad was stuck with them. His dad got a call asking if he would like to bid on them and so they did. The bid was accepted and that got them into the nut business. It became a multimillion dollar business called Los Angeles Nut house.

My relationship with Eddie began through business transactions. We kind of hit it off because we thought pretty much alike. He was of a positive nature and so was I. No pun intended that this was where the *cans* and the *can'ts* came into the picture again.

He gave me many ideas on merchandising and selling various commodities unknown to the retail trade at the time. I will talk about this more later, but our business relationship and our personal relationship were miles apart. If his price wasn't right, we skipped over him and if what he sold us didn't meet our quality standards, then merchandise was rejected and sent back to him. There are not too many opportunities to strike up that sort of relationship. Here again is where the true friend part comes to play.

I remember one day in particular when Eddie and I were discussing things in general, and you all know how that goes, one thing leads to another. We happened to be on the subject of families because we were both members of large families and we were family-oriented. He made the statement to me, "Gene, I tell you things that I don't even tell my brothers." It was so wonderful to be able to do business with a person and still have freedom to share non-business feelings, ideas, thoughts or beliefs. Eddie was Jewish and I was Italian, and we would tell each other about our various nationality customs. Where we really had a sound foundation is when it came to respect and dignity. We respected each other and we dignified one another and when things had to be said they were said in the manner that the other side could accept as a genuine concern minus any ridicule.

During our time that we were associated with each other I had several deaths occurring within my family group. We lost our dear mother, dear dad, a brother, mother-in-law and a sister-in-law. I also had a couple of major surgeries and suffered one bout of complete exhaustion and had to be off the job for several months. Eddie always found time to be there when the chips were down.

When my brother Al passed away, one of his daughters, Joni, was graduating from high school in San Diego. I had mentioned that I had to go down there for her graduation. Eddie's comment was, "Gene, if you don't mind I'd sure like to go with you. I'd love to see her graduate."

Eddie passed away about 20 years ago but he shall always be in my mind and my heart because he was a great human being. The number of people at Eddie's funeral was well into the hundreds, which was further evidence of how great a guy he was. I believe the nicest thing a guy like Eddie leaves us is this: so many people remember his kindness and it becomes a part of their way of life. Remembering Edward brings to my mind the Confucius saying, *I hear and I forget, I see and I remember, I do and I understand. Don't talk about it – do it.*

This concludes my chapter on my dearest friends.

Chapter 10
UNUSUAL HAPPENINGS IN MY LIFETIME
SOME PLEASANT ONES,
SOME NOT SO PLEASANT

You have no doubt all heard the story about *THE LITTLE ENGINE THAT COULD*, which tells how a blue locomotive engine carrying a load of toys overcomes formidable obstacles, a towering mountain by repeating to itself these words, *I think I can, I think I can, I think I can.* That is what this chapter is all about, and it coincides with the title of this book, *success come in cans, failure comes in can'ts.* I am here to tell you that success can also come in can'ts. I can't do that because it's not the right thing to do. Hopefully we learn from our experience. It certainly taught me a great lesson. Winston Churchill told us that success is going from failure to failure without the loss of enthusiasm.

As I stated several times, this book is about my real life, good, bad, indifferent etc. with the main goal of always learning and moving forward. My mom used to tell me to do good and forget it, because doing bad in the memory will linger. At the age of about 12, a school buddy and I decided we wanted to hit the road, so hit the road we did. We hitched a freight car in South Chicago that took us to Morris, Illinois, 65 miles away from home. The local sheriff saw us walking down the street and being strangers, he questioned us. He soon found out we were runaways, called our home, put us on a train and headed us back to Chicago. Upon returning home and seeing and hearing my mom's crying and sobbing made me really feel shameful of my horrible hurt that I imposed on her. From that day forward until the day she left this world, there was nothing I would not do for her. It is difficult for me to even write about this thoughtless plan of mine. I believe that this fiasco brought me closer to God. Praise God for his grace and guidance. I believe that was my greatest mistake of my life, and I shed tears as I write this. Another antic that I've got involved in with a friend was when I was in between jobs and this friend asked me if I would like a kind of a part-time job doing phone work. The phone work turned out to be a bookie phone man. The office was located across the street from the main gate at Santa Anita racetrack.

All I had to do was take the phone calls from clients. They had a number like M 34, they would give me the necessary information, such as five dollars to win on Brown Derby, fifth race, Santa Anita racetrack. It wasn't quite my cup of tea so I gave up on it pretty early. I was amazed to discover the number of people in my general neighborhood who bet on horses through bookmakers.

On another occasion, I had a friend who was a realtor in a development of a large commercial project. He offered me his share in the company, but my finances couldn't meet the price. So I asked if I could pass the info on to a friend and he agreed. The friend invested and got his share back on the first sale; he later told me he had already made over several hundred thousand dollars and still had half the project to be sold. Needless to say, I was very happy for him. He had promised us a world tour but he passed away and his family forgot all about us. It was then that I recalled my mom's words: do good and forget about it, your life and mine will be valued not by what we take but by what we give.

Chapter 11
IF YOU HAVE YOUR HEALTH,
YOU HAVE IT ALL

On living well, take care of your body as if you're going to live forever, take care of your soul as if you were going to die tomorrow. Excellent advice but we don't all adhere to it.

I have been a very active person all my life. I worked a lot, played a lot, did my share of drinking and in between I tried my best to adhere to those things that kept me healthy. At the age of three I had my tonsils removed. I do remember getting out of bed, walking in the hallway looking for my mother and I must've exerted myself because I vomited in the hallway, which made the nurses very unhappy.

My health was fairly decent through most of my life and finally at the age of 59, I began to have some complications. For starters I had a perforated ulcer. I kept working and bleeding for three days at which time I was rushed to emergency with a hemoglobin down to three. Normal is about 14. At any rate they did the surgery, I came out fine and went about my merry way of doing everything that I should do and more. Then along came a heart attack and a three way bypass. Then 10 years later came another bypass, this time a five way. In between, for excitement I fell out of a tree, went into a coma and as a result of the fall, I lost my sense of taste and smell, which has never returned.

Throughout the years I've had four stints put into my veins and in 2014 I had a defibrillator wired to my heart. Did I mention that I had a nervous breakdown in 1970 that resulted in a recouping period of about six months?

I will be 92 years old in January of this year, 2016. I look and feel good. I am active with my church activities. I also am a great gardener. I do a lot of gardening from April through September each year. I give my thanks to Jesus for seeing me through these 92 years, for he has told us, and I believe it, "I can do all things through Christ who strengthens me." Philippians 4: 13

Here's a typical day's activity is for me. I arise at 5:00 A.M., spend an hour praying, attend daily mass at 7:30 A.M., visit homebound people practically every day, make phone calls of encouragement to those who are ill, depressed, lonely, bedridden. My visits include reading and praying one on one, conversation, listening, errand boy, and so forth.

I strongly believe that one person caring about another represents life's greatest values.

I believe I mentioned earlier that I attended training at Loyola University, the Stephen Ministry course. It's a great course that involves care-giving for those who are living with different types of problems that life can present to us, such as depression, suicide, grieving, job loss, hospitalization, terminal illness, religious matters, divorce etc. It's a great program designed to assist those in need of love and care. I also visit patients in our local hospital one day per week, bringing them communion or praying with them or merely visiting. The usual day is approximately 50 to 60 patients.

My beautiful wife Gloria is most understanding, praise the Lord. Although I am gone part of the time I continue to care for her wants and needs as they occur.

It's amazing what a person can accomplish with the help of determination, enthusiasm and love for others. Helping others has taught me this; people do not care how much you know until they know how much you care. This may sound repetitive of what I write about in this book, but it is truly life as I really know it and lived.

Chapter 12
THE PRODUCE BUSINESS - MY CAREER

I have spoken much about my involvement in the produce business. It's something that I fell in love with from the very start. There's not too much that I can say that would be contrary to the produce business that I love. What do I like about the produce business? I love the beautiful colors of the fruits and vegetables, the many different ways of displaying the items and the importance of produce items as nutritional food. Many items change with the seasons. Each season brings its particular group of items to the market. There is much to learn about produce. The number of varieties of items, the best growing area for specific items, if it's a perishable item. It keeps you on your toes by staying on top of quantities ordered, proper storage, proper handling, these all play a big part in the produce business. You are dealing with a perishable commodity that is most desired by the public and as we used to say, "Eye appeal is buy appeal."

I am inclined to be artistic with produce items and clothes. I do not say this in a boastful way; it just comes natural for me. I use my imagination and picture what, where, quantity, type of display, decorations etc. Once the picture is clear in my mind, I go to work and produce it. I do the same scenario with wearing apparel. I can walk through my closet and pick out the suit coat, trousers, shirt and tie and the match is perfect. I also have a similar talent with numbers. While others are crunching numbers in their calculators, I am crunching numbers in my head, while they are still punching numbers.

I have always had a photographic mind and a good memory. As for the memory part, I love music. I remember song titles and the words from the songs of the 1920s and 30s. My mind has been a great asset to me and at times a hindrance, but I thank God for both the asset and the hindrance. It's a matter of using the right one the most, at the proper time.

My produce career began when I sold produce from my uncle's truck. Then my brother Al and I began a produce business on our own with our home-built wagon. From there I got involved in the supermarket industry. What I will be sharing here is the ups and downs of my produce career with a national food chain where I spent 30 years of my produce career.

It was fun, but it was a lot of hard work. It had many rewards and long hours and I like to say that it taught me a lot about people, which I consider the most valuable information to any human being.

I do not recall if I mentioned earlier, but I always felt that what helped me the most in life was getting to know more about people. You might know all there is to know about apples and oranges, bananas, etc., but if you do not know how to carry that information to others then the knowledge loses its value.

When it comes to people, I would put this in a very simple manner. It's knowing what to say, how to say it, when to say it, why to say it. In today's world so much time is spent on idle and useless conversation, which is completely non-productive.

Give this idea some thought; everything you do or say at some point is going to involve another human being. So street smarts or time on the firing line or people knowledge comes into play big time. There are many college graduates who are not where they would like to be after spending four years in college. Job wise, that is. When I was discharged from the Marines I accepted a job as produce department manager with a national food chain. I enjoyed the work and I did well. We had what we called open-front stores. We had to roll out the food stands to face the sidewalk. The food stands were partially on the sidewalk and we rolled down an awning for protection from sun or rain.

It wasn't long before my reputation and my innovation of display methods spread throughout the district. Other store managers were asking their Produce Department Managers to stop in my store and take a look at our method of operation, and that went on for several months. Before long there came promotions to larger produce departments with greater sales. I was receiving calls from the order department challenging me on the quantities that I was ordering. I remember a call from the order department one day and they asked if I really wanted thirty boxes of artichokes or was that a mistake. My answer was, "Yes, I do. Send them out." The same thing occurred when I ordered twenty units of broccoli, but here again, I would picture in my mind a huge display of a given commodity, and of course I made certain that the quality was extremely good and the weather was in my favor. I selected a good spot for display and I would say to myself, when they see this much product on display they will stop and buy some. I believe that's where picturing things in your mind gives you an edge over the other guy. Please don't misunderstand me; I have had many pictures in my mind where I had to hit the reject button, because they just didn't sound or look like the right thing to do.

We talk about our body and how much it does for us, but what the body does depends a lot on what the mind tells it to do. I am certain most people are aware of this, but I am equally certain that many people do not receive the full potential of their mental capacity. As stated earlier it has worked wonders for me. To put it very simply, my mind gave me pictures of what I was trying to accomplish, and all I had to do was put my body to work and reproduce what was in that picture. Sounds simple and it is.

As time went on, the company I worked for decided to add produce instructors throughout the division and I was selected as one of the instructors. But I am getting a little ahead of myself.

Each time I would go shopping with my wife in one of our stores, or occasionally into a competitor's store, I would point out the various things in the Produce Department that were not producing the desired results, and how with some minor changes things could be much more profitable.

I even went so far as to tell her on many occasions, "Gloria, I envision myself going from store to store within our company, showing Produce Department Managers display techniques, season displays, featured items. Items that produce the most profit, proper handling, proper processing, mainly the vegetables." I had that picture in my mind day after day. Now I can get back to being selected as a produce instructor. The picture in my mind came to fruition and now for the rest of the story as my role as a Produce Instructor.

Before I continue my experience as a Produce Instructor, I would like to share a thought that came to my mind regarding desire for achievement. My desire for achievement never had any monetary strings attached to it. I merely had a desire to come up with thoughts, ideas, plans, etc. that were better than the other guys.

One day while reading one of my religious books I came across the word *enthusiasm* and what I was reading went on to say that the word is taken from the Greek word *Enthuse,* meaning God within. How interesting I thought, because I included God in all my plans and asked for the Holy Spirit to guide me in all that I do, think and say.

Even at my age of 92, I maintain a daily schedule of activity from 5 A.M. to 10 P.M. Although much of my activity is not of a physical nature it nevertheless requires much energy. People ask me how I keep going at such a torrid rate day in and day out. I always have the same standard answer. It is not I who maintains this schedule; it is the Holy Spirit that moves me to and fro.

Now back to my experience as a produce instructor, and here's where the fun begins. As a Produce Department Manager Instructor it was my job to have each trainee personally involved physically and mentally in each phase of managing a Produce Department. The training included training vessels, doing what we call "crisping" leafy vegetables before displaying, proper display techniques, display allocation based on seasonal demand items, color scheme affect for displays. Grouping items together that required moisture and those items that should be kept away from moisture. Balanced ordering, recording total losses from spoilage, recording losses from reduced prices, supportive advertised items, inventory of stock monthly, schedule work hours for personnel and display maintenance and proper storage and handling of all items.

The training course lasted for six days. Monday through Saturday, occasionally it was for 12 days depending on the trainees requirements.

My first trainee was a gentleman named Bill Decker. I mention his name because we're still close friends; he is 95 years of age. Bill and his wife Fauvette have been married for 70 years. We spent many years together in the produce business. Bill became a Produce Instructor for our company nationwide.

As I continued with the Produce Department Training course, word got around to the Southern California area about the success of the program. It was common for produce meetings to be held in the evening at our Produce Department after regular store hours. I received many compliments from upper management and from Produce Department Managers as well as from produce clerks who would drop in our store for a look see.

I refer back to mentioning to my wife that I could see myself going from store to store assisting Produce Department Managers by showing them a better way of operating their produce departments.

You no doubt have heard the old saying of the law of attraction; you are a living magnet and you invariably attract into your life people, situations and circumstances that are in harmony with your dominant thoughts. I truly believe this and I have since I was a youngster. As a youngster I was taught to treat my fellow humans with love and respect. I was reminded that if you were blessed with good looks, abundance of brains, born into wealthy family or blessed in other ways and means, what you had that was an abundance of talent was not to use to your advantage only. It was given to you by God to be shared with others. It brings much happiness to you when you share your God-given talent.

Failure comes in cants, success comes in cans. Remember this, as you ponder the above saying. Enthusiasm is God within. Failures? Sure, we all have them at times. Listen to this information on yesterday today and tomorrow. Yesterday is gone, it's history. Tomorrow's not here yet. Who knows what tomorrow may bring? Today is all we have to work with. We may use today to repair the damage from yesterday's mistakes. We may use yesterday's mistakes for future reference to look back and avoid making the same mistake over again. Use today to organize a plan for tomorrow. Experience is not what happens to a person. It's what a person does with the experience that happens to them.

I remember my mother telling me that nothing is small in the eyes of God. Do everything with love. I remembered her words well and I love the produce business. I love training people; all that I did, I did with love and enthusiasm. Let me repeat once again, monetary gain was not my main propellant. Self-accomplishment, overcoming challenges and moving on to new challenges was my main motivation.

Not expecting further advancement, but doing the best job possible, where I was at the time was my ambition. When we stay focused on the job at hand, things come together smoothly. Evidently others thought that my training program produced the desired results. There was talk about adding a produce consultant to the main office staff.

At the time they had one produce consultant on staff for the entire division, which included 14 districts. They were looking to add a second produce consultant so that each consultant would have half of the division or seven districts each under their supervision. They had nominated several candidates and I was selected as one of them.

I was asked to appear in the employment relations department office for an aptitude test. I showed up for the test and did well. I was told that my IQ was equal to a two-year college person.

I accepted the assignment and to me it was a real challenge. I would be conducting district meetings, working with Produce Department

Managers, rewriting division policy for produce personnel, establishing procedure for produce personnel, such as writing a produce manual, promoting special events and so forth.

I must relate my experience with the consultant that was already on staff. I was asked to spend a period of time with him and in general spent some time learning and reviewing his assignments, as my assignments would be much the same as his.

There are first week's assignments where we were scheduled to be out of town and that meant staying at motels until we visited all the stores that were on our schedule. About three days out of town we visited a store in Kern County. The Produce Department Manager was obviously having a problem operating his department successfully. The consultant that was breaking me in was either trying to impress me or perhaps he had tried helping this manager on a previous occasion, but results were not showing up.

To make a long story short, this poor Produce Department Manager was in tears when we left the store and he kept saying he would try harder and that he needed the job very badly. That evening after dinner we went back to our motel rooms and the first thing I did when I got back to my room was to call my wife and tell her, I don't think I like this new job. I relayed the incident of the Produce Department Manager who we left in tears at our last store visit. I remember tossing in bed that night and after a while I fell asleep and thank God I awoke with a new thought in mind. That's not the way I'm going to operate as a consultant. I know I can do better than that. This is where, control my lifeline, not an anchor makes a lot of sense, so I chalked the whole thing to experience.

To continue on with the same scenario of the Produce Department Manager in tears, a thought crossed my mind. What does a shopper look for in a Produce Department? FRESH PRODUCE. What follows is BINGO. I put my thought to work before my next store visit. What follows is a thought that I came up with.

I received a call from the district office from a certain store that was having some serious loss of produce sales. Upon entering the store after the usual greeting, the reason for my visit, so forth with the Produce Department Manager I suggested the following, let's get a shopping cart and shop your produce department. Each item on display I would select what I thought was an item that a customer would not purchase. Then I would ask the produce department manager this question. "If you were shopping here today, would you purchase this?" The answer was, "no." Then we would replace the item in the shopping cart. We went through every display in his department and at the end of our shopping trip we had a pretty full basket of customer rejected items. My comment to the produce department manager was, could this be the answer why your sales are on the decline? My recommendation to him was to start a pre-display culling program. In other words, if you wouldn't buy it, do not put it on display. Even if you are working from a box of merchandise from new stock, there are some items that got by the packers. U.S. number one is 85% to

95% so that means some items in the container are questionable. As the place sells down, the 15% or 5% become more pronounced.

I used the same theme in other store visits and it worked well. No tears, no fuss. All one had to do was get their head out of their ass so they could see what they were doing.

I am a great believer in making certain that whoever I am teaching or giving instructions to, or in simple terms, as they are to learn something from me and my mind, I want to be sure of the following. They understand, they are committed, they participate, accept well intended criticism. In other words their full participation, heart and soul. I am amazed how much parents do for their children nowadays. To raise the family is a real challenge. It takes the full cooperation of both parents. I guess the best way to say it is that children learn by example. They must be taught that to get benefits in life, they must earn them.

It brings to mind my assignment as a Eucharistic minister to a local hospital and a portion of the patients I visited were in the maternity ward. When I entered a new mother's room, I would elaborate on the excitement, the glory, the honor, the beautiful feeling and God's blessing to be able to reproduce a human being and as usual and rightfully so, tears were related. I would inform them that along with the glory of having a child comes responsibilities. What little Suzy wears, what she eats, what she says and how she said it, and what she does are going to be your responsibility. As the late Bishop Sheen so nicely stated, if you have not taught your child the basic fundamentals of life by the age of six, you have waited too long.

I recall that our two boys were not doing a good job on the yard work as they should have and those days I would have meetings about once a month with all of the family. The main purpose of the meeting was to discuss happenings within the family, good, bad or indifferent. It was good therapy and we learned a lot about each other and we shared our pros and cons of events within the family and outside of the family. At this particular meeting I challenged the boys on the results of their yard work which was below par. So I politely stated that beginning next week, the two boys would be doing dishes, setting the table and fixing beds and the girls would do the outside work. Psychologically it was very effective. It's important for children to know that we care about them in every respect.

I didn't mean to deviate from my produce story but there is a human element that I wanted to get in there.

What it all boils down to in management is that "managers" are probably the most loosely used words in America. In the dictionary *manager* means to bring about success, accomplishing, to take charge of, to take care of, the dominator, to influence, to handle, direct, control in action or use, to contrive when to get along. In other words, the managers are responsible for much. To site one more scenario, when my wife and I became Guardian for my brother's children, there was a period of time when our car insurance policy had two adults and seven teenagers on it. The company canceled us out and said we had to go to high-risk insurance. Well, we did, and so did the teenagers, and as we told them then and it's still true today, responsibility builds character.

I enjoyed my new assignment as a produce consultant immensely. There were approximately 80 stores in my seven districts. Between district meetings, division and individual store contacts, I had plenty to do to satisfy my desire for achievement. I love my work and I love the people I work with.

I did have my embarrassing moments though. There was this one district meeting that I was to speak at that I shall always remember. I had prepared thoroughly and completely. It was one of my first meetings that I held shortly after I was promoted to produce consultant. I stood before the group of about 50 produce personnel and my mind went completely blank. I was so embarrassed that I had all I could do to keep from shedding tears. But as the old saying goes, "It's not how many times you fall that counts, it's the number of times that you get up." I was fortunate to have the district manager come to my rescue. It was also a good lesson for me. I learned that when you speak before a group, be yourself, stand up, speak up, and then shut up.

As I stated several times on previous pages of this book, enthusiasm, desire, commitment, all are good driving forces.

I continued doing my best in my new assignment as produce consultant and after a period of about two years I received a call from the overall merchandising manager to show up for an appointment. No mention was made of the reason for the appointment. One can get all kinds of thoughts in a situation such as this one I just described.

Nevertheless, it was July 3, I remember the date because our stores were closed on July 4. When I got to the appointment I was told that my performance as a produce consultant was excellent. I was asked if would I consider leaving the position to become a produce buyer. A kind of special produce buyer for our problem stores. Problems stores were stores that produced less than desired sales and/or profits for various reasons. The real estate department made many poor site selections for the location, tough competition moved into the area, occasionally there was personnel problems. My job was to walk the late produce market in Los Angeles and look for special buys on produce for the selected problem stores.

The gentleman that interviewed me said I wouldn't have to answer right then, I could go home and discuss with my wife and let him know my reply on July 5.

My reply on the spot was, I accept, there is no need to talk to my wife. She has already proved her support on all my employment decisions and that's exactly what happened when I told my wife, my little Angel from heaven, about the new offer. Her comment was, "If you think you'll like it, it's fine with me." I might add at this point it's still the same after 66 years of marriage.

As I engaged in my new assignment, and it was a rather difficult one to say the least, we were able to get special buys but they were not utilized as they were intended to be. Some stores did not lower the price on the item, so they could increase their profits. Some stores failed to put the item on display quickly and other stores decided the item was not the right one for their trade area. To sum it up, discipline was lacking. In a program of this kind, follow-through is a must, and due to the lack of follow-through and the inability to closely supervise the program because of distance between stores we recommended that the program be discontinued. I however continued on with the special buying program but with a different approach. As special buys were made they were offered to stores in general on a rotation basis.

I continued on with this special assignment under the leadership of a man that held the position called Produce Supply Manager and meantime I was familiarizing myself with the backstage operation of our division, supply, trucking, warehousing, advertising, etc.

I felt as though I was situated in a rather unusual position. Here I was working the L. A. produce market for special buys and spending time on the phone finding homes for the special buys. Not exactly boring but a rather different routine than I had in the past. I remember the wise words of my mother, do good no matter what you are doing, and so I did my best and continued on.

It seemed as though the upper management still had plans for me because one morning after my L. A. market work was completed, I headed for the office. I was sitting at my desk when the overall Merchandising Manager came into my office and said, "Gene, what do you say we go get a cup of coffee in the cafeteria?" Here, I wondered again as I had in the past, what this cup of coffee would lead up to.

My reason for the concern was because this fellow and I had words while he was head of the trucking department. One of our stores had requested a truck of bananas. He was not in the position to handle such a request. I proceeded to advise him how it could be handled well with very little extra effort. At any rate it was approved by the Retail Operations Manager. Needless to say it was not much to his liking.

Back to the cup of coffee with the Merchandising Manager. He explained to me that they were creating a new title for the head of the retail produce operations and the title would be Produce Merchandising Manager. The present person in charge of produce operations and produce supply manager would respond to the Produce Merchandising Manager. After he explained the responsibilities that went with the new title, they included produce sales, produce profits, produce pricing, weekly add items, produce fixtures, layouts for new stores and remodels, attend weekly staff meetings, supervise produce consultants (one for each district), attend monthly profit and loss meetings with the staff and a few other extras from time to time.

This was a big step forward, more than I had ever undertaken. More than anyone in the company had ever undertaken. I was the youngest at age 34 to hold that position within the company nationwide, but I accepted and explained that it would be quite a challenge. I would kind of have to grow into the job.

To this day, I don't think they realized that the move from the position of Produce Department Manager to that of Produce Operations in less than five years is moving up rather quickly.

At any rate, I accepted the position but my main concern was about the man who was now at the helm. He had been on the job for about 20 years and was only three years away from retirement. My question was had he been told yet? The answer was no. You and I are going to tell him now.

I had heard that corporations deal harshly in matters such as these. We proceeded to meet with the Produce Supply Manager and all the facts were presented to him, not a word to me and I shall always remember the look on his face as the facts were explained to him. At the end of the day I went home and relayed all the days happening to my little angel from heaven, including my feeling for the man I was replacing. She agreed, but she said they could not have picked a better man for the job. God bless her.

I am happy to report this though, I immediately sat down with the Produce Supply Manager and told him I needed him and what a great job he had done through all those years and that I would continue to respect his input and my treatment of him would always be respectful, and rightfully so. He deserved it and he earned it. I mentioned to him that we might not agree on everything, but when everything is said and done, my decision or yours is we give it our all, and he agreed.

He retired after three years of working with me. We had a nice retirement party for him and I was so pleased to hear him tell me these words, "Gene, the last three years with this company were the best years I had, working with you."

Had I thought I had a lot of excitement up to this point moving up the ladder, I was wrong, because I really did not realize the challenges that lay ahead. The merchandising of produce within our company was still patterned after the 1930's and 40's plan.

Farmers were still delivering produce on open truck in hot weather. In some cases water was still on vegetables from watering or from rain. So I zeroed in on point of origin to start with: who, what, where, when, why and how.

If we had good suppliers bringing in good products, that was a good start. Secondly, was the product being handled after we received it at our warehouse? We could lose what we gained on step one if our warehousing and trucking departments were not giving the proper care to the products.

Last but not least, how were we showing the product to our customers at store level? We already had the store personnel set on a good training program. We had not arrived yet but were making good strides in the right direction.

So that was basically the program I had set up for them to follow. There were a lot of knobs to turn, people to convince, some confrontation but no different than life anywhere else on this earth. So that's what I will be addressing in the remaining portion of this chapter.

* * *

An unfinished labor of love.........

Gene died May 28th, 2016, and as much as he wanted to, he did not have time to finish his book. We printed what he had done so far, and hope you enjoy what he wrote. One never knows what tomorrow will bring. We never thought of him having cancer in the lung. It was a very aggressive type of cancer, and he lasted only about ten days after we found out. He had been in the hospital, and when he came home with Hospice, he declined very rapidly.

Regardless of what he had in life, he had the will and the courage to go on. At the age of 65, he got a real estate license, an insurance license, notary license, and other financial licenses. He never quit learning and trying other financial sources.

He loved his family and was very proud of everyone in it, including all the spouses who married into it. We have a beautiful family and have to thank God. He has been so generous, kind and loving to all of us.

Gene loved to do volunteer work in the church, in the hospital, and visited many people who were homebound. He was in Hospice for many years, and taught Stephen Ministry classes at church for about ten years. We drove people to church every Sunday, made coffee at church, and sold Scrip once a month, until his death.

"You have been the most kind, caring and loving husband for 66 years, and I was proud to have you as my husband. You did everything with all of your heart and soul. You were a good father, grandfather, great grandfather for 56 people in our family."

"Thank you my dear Gene, I will be with you someday soon. I miss you very much, I will always love you."

Your loving wife, Gloria.

By Sam Calvano

So I read the book to the very end. It ended too soon. Uncle Gene is gone and it would not be finished.

I got the idea one day that I should write about him to finish the book. And maybe some other family members would do the same.

When I was a kid spending summers in Duarte, Uncle Gene and family lived three houses down from Uncle Art's house on Duncannon. Sundays were big days on Duncannon. Aunty Mary and Uncle Bussy lived across from Uncle Art, Aunt Theresa and Uncle Greg lived next door to Uncle Bussy, Auntie Ida and Uncle Pepe lived down the street. Grandma and Grandpa Calvano lived one block over on Cotter.

On a particular Sunday, Uncle Gene and family were at Uncle Bussy's in the front yard. Kids were running around and his youngest daughter Mary was dressed in a cute little dress. They were going somewhere.

Uncle Gene was always going somewhere. With family or for work, but always on the move.

While still living on Duncannon he bought a brand new '58 Chevy. I was older and had started to develop an interest in cars. His was a 4-door beige Biscayne.

Fast forward a couple of years and I was living with Auntie Ida. One day Uncle Gene stopped by her house in a brand new '60 Chevy Impala 4-door hardtop. What made this car special was that it had air conditioning. A very rare option in 1960.

Uncle Gene and Aunt Gloria had moved to Glendora by this time into a nice house. Going to visit was always a blast because I could play with my two cousins, Pete and Dom.

Fast forward again to 1961 and my sisters and I were reunited in San Diego. Family visits from the relatives in Los Angeles were a welcome treat, especially when it was Uncle Gene and family. They would come down on Saturday and stay through Sunday. Saturday night was always fun because Uncle Gene and my dad would start the evening off with some beers, would play the accordion, sing, laugh and just have a grand ole time. Sunday rolled around and we all said our goodbyes. Happy they were there but sad to see them go.

One of those visits brought them down in a new '63 Pontiac Bonneville convertible. It was white, beautiful and loaded with optional equipment such as power windows, tilt steering wheel, power seats and more.

The next time I saw Uncle Gene was at Nick and Rose Ann's wedding. Lots of beer for the adults, lots of fun, and sugary treats for the kids. Uncle Gene was driving a new '65 Pontiac Grand Prix. Apparently that Pontiac was not a favorite. His next family trip to San Diego was in a new '65 Olds 98 convertible. Pete and I played in that car for a long time, comparing it to my dad's Plymouth convertible. That Olds was a beautiful car.

I had a feeling Uncle Gene made more money than my dad. It didn't make any difference when they were together. They had fun. Being around Uncle Gene was always fun. No business, just fun.

And then one day my sisters' and my life changed in about three seconds. My dad was severely injured in a freak accident. Rosemary, the drunken stepmother, did not know what to do except to call Uncle Gene. That was the best thing she ever did for my sisters and me.

It is not a clear memory of exactly when Uncle Gene showed up. That '65 Olds was suddenly on the street in front of our house and it was such a relief to see it. Uncle Gene was here!

From the moment of his arrival I saw a different man. He was analyzing the situation, keeping calm, making plans, visiting my unconscious father in the hospital and giving us hope. This was a new Uncle Gene! He brought order to a chaotic situation. Something I found out as time went by that he was very good at doing.

Uncle Gene had made a commitment to my dad that he would watch over us in the unlikely event that something happened to my dad. Uncle Gene took commitments seriously, as I found out as time went by, and his commitment to watch over his brother's children was unwavering.

I had just turned fifteen and needed a job. Uncle Gene had the answer. I would be a box boy at Safeway. I got the job and was admonished before my first day of work to NEVER call in sick with a cold. I never did. Commitment!

Six months later on July 4th, 1967, three of my sisters and I reunited in an apartment in San Diego.

Uncle Gene made all the arrangements in one trip to San Diego to set us up and we moved down.

Fast forward again to 1969. My sister Roe needed a car to get to work. Uncle Gene arrived in San Diego and proceeded to help her make the purchase of a used Mustang. The next day he took my sister Rita to the same dealer and said she needed a newer car too. The deal was made within a short period and off Rita drove in her car.

The building we lived in was on a corner. I was used to seeing the Olds parked on the side street when Uncle Gene was visiting. One day I was dropped off at home after work and saw a brand new '68 Bonneville on the street. It didn't even have plates on it but I knew it was Uncle Gene's. At first, I thought WOW, what a cool car. Then fear crept in and I started wondering why he suddenly showed up unannounced. He only did that when he felt something was amiss or someone had done something wrong. I entered the apartment with trepidation. Phew!!! It was just a routine visit. Although there was a short conversation about me smoking cigarettes. His question to me about smoking was: "Can you afford it?" I was working and only smoking a pack a week, so I said yes. His immediate response was something to the effect that he wasn't talking about the money but the health issues. Problem was that he was still smoking and so did not present a convincing argument.

On another visit he found out I used hairspray on my hair to keep it in place. He made a remark about that which intimated that men did not do that. Imagine my surprise one day when visiting at his house a couple of years later and I saw him in the bathroom with this plastic thing on his head. He was dyeing his hair! I continued to use hair spray.

Eventually I needed a car. Uncle Gene's best friend Eddie just happened to have one that his salesman had used. I bought the car for $500.00. I was to pay Uncle Gene $50.00 per month until it was paid off. One month I missed a payment. He cornered me one day and I received a huge lecture that centered around what else? Commitment! I was never late again.

Three years passed and I wanted to move from San Diego. I mentioned this to Uncle Gene. He queried me as to where I wanted to move. Lake Tahoe, Las Vegas, or Los Angeles. "You are moving to LA". "You will live with us." Although under age at the time, I resisted and eventually moved into an apartment in Monrovia.

Shortly after the move Uncle Gene bought his first Cadillac. Triple black and a convertible too. He sold me the Bonneville and carried the note again. I never missed a payment.

After the move I spent more time with Uncle Gene on the weekends and occasionally went to a business dinner with him. The dinners were always at nice restaurants. Business was discussed and deals were made over a steak, a cigarette and VO on the rocks with a twist. That is still one of my favorite meals, minus the cigarettes of course.

Even though Uncle Gene was my role model, I think every young man has to rebel against their father or in this case against the father figure. Uncle Gene and I had a difference of opinion on my reaction to a situation at Safeway. I went to his house one night to discuss how it should be handled. His response was not what I thought it would be and I left angry and depressed. Not so depressed that I didn't call my lawyer immediately and tell him to take the case. Uncle Gene called me one afternoon, prompted by a call to him from the head of employee relations. Safeway had received a cease and desist letter from my lawyer explaining the ramifications of their actions toward me. I was still angry at him and played dumb when asked what was going on. I asked what he was referring to and then explained that I did what he suggested and if Safeway did not cease their actions against me I would proceed with legal action against the company.

It was a decisive moment in my life. I had taken a stand against a person I loved for what I thought was right. The incident changed my relationship with him. I was not his equal but I felt I was on more equal footing with him from then on. As I look back on the incident now, it was probably embarrassing for him to receive that call from employee relations, but in the seven or so years since he took legal custody of me he had trained me to make decisions by watching him, so I made a decision. I would like to think that he was okay with me making the decision and that I stood up for myself. If he wasn't okay with it he never said so. A few years later he found out that I had been vindicated of the accusation.

I wanted to emulate Uncle Gene. When eating out I ordered steak dinners at good restaurants, I smoked cigarettes, I drank one of his favorite liquors, Seagrams VO, stayed in nice hotels when I travelled, bought expensive shoes, and after I totaled the Bonneville, bought my first Cadillac. It was the same color as his. I also wanted to marry someone just like the person he married. I also wanted to make deals like he did.

Safeway had other plans for me that were not going to get me to the job that would be like Uncle Gene's so I made the decision to change careers. Not too long after my departure Uncle Gene was ousted from Safeway.

Not one to sit around and lick his wounds, Uncle Gene and Aunt Gloria moved to Apple Valley, CA, and bought a house across the street from their daughter Annie. He started making plans to build his own produce store in Victorville. He bought the land, made the plans and got the place built. While plans and building were going on he started selling produce off a truck across the street from where the store was being built. I asked him why sell now. Basically, he said it was good advertising for the new store because it got people excited.

The few times I visited him while the store was being built I was volunteered for work on the construction, as were all my cousins. Ah well, if it helps the old uncle, why not?

His dream became a reality on Grand Opening weekend. All the relatives came up from "down below" to check it out. I was put to work behind the deli counter. The counter was an old used refrigerated box with many wood doors that had some very shiny hardware. They were heavy to open. The place was jumping! The deli department was nonstop. I was thinking about taking a short break when Uncle Gene showed up, told me to come around to the front of the case so he could point out that the case did not look good because it needed to be faced. I thought "damn, this is just like when I was in produce at Safeway". He was right, but I was too tired to care. Not so tired that I didn't go back and straighten up that case though and keep it faced until my shift ended. How could a person say they were tired when you knew that he had risen at three or four in the morning and stayed until the job was done? You couldn't.

He was committed.

The store was a success. He added on a new deli and eating area. He bought the property next door. And then all of a sudden, he gave the business to his kids and he moved to Indio to run a date farm.

Let's not forget the cars. I had a small accident in his first Eldorado. I took him to the airport on the west side of LAX so he could fly to Tahoe for a Safeway meeting. Remember now that I loved emulating him. Despite the cold I put the top down. Paying little attention to the car in front of me at a stoplight I hit it. There was some damage unseen by me but pointed out by Aunt Gloria later. I knew I was in big trouble. He got home and reviewed the damage with me, gave me the lecture and then told me he would pay for it. What just happened here? I wrecked his car, he was angry with me and then he paid to get it fixed?? It was a lesson in forgiveness.

So, there was another Eldo convertible, an Eldo coupe, a Buick Park Avenue, a Buick Limited, an Olds 88 and somewhere in there a surprise car. A big Mazda. Which he also wrecked.

The demise of the Bushel Basket business after the store was transferred to the children was a huge financial blow to Uncle Gene and Aunt Gloria.

Forgiveness. Again.

He never placed blame for the problem and he paid all the store debts. He now had very little savings and very little income. Safeway had a way of removing employees at all levels when many were close to retirement. It saved a lot of money for the company so there was only a pittance of funds from that source and social security. He needed to have additional income and so...

"Success comes in cans."

Uncle Gene was not one who took adversity lying down. Next thing I knew, he was a licensed real estate agent, a licensed investment counselor, and a licensed insurance agent. He was also originating real estate loans. After a while he exited the real estate business and concentrated on insurance products and real estate lending. There was a short stint with an energy company and an equally short time with a pyramid insurance company. He did well. He and Aunt Gloria were able to buy another home.

Let's take a break here and talk about cars. There was one car that I loathed. A Nissan *something*. It was painted the color of Apple Valley dirt. I hated to see him in it. One day I called him and asked when he could come to San Diego. He asked why and when I told him I couldn't tell him on the phone, being the good Italian that he was, he only asked if he could bring Aunt Gloria. The next morning, they arrived at my office on time. They were never late for anything. After the hi how are ya's were over I told them to follow me in that ugly car. We pulled up in front of the Pontiac dealer and on the showroom floor was a brand-new car, huge bow and all, with their name on it. I told him that if he wanted the car he had to leave the ugly one with me. They did. And about a year or so later he totaled that one too. He called me to tell me about it. I think he thought I would be angry about the loss. My first thought though was when I damaged the Eldo and he forgave me.

And what did he do on his off time? He became more deeply involved with the local Catholic church and was trained as a Stephens minister to go around and listen to other people's problems. All of this at a time when many people a decade younger than he was would have completely retired. He did not reduce his church activities until he was in his nineties and was told to slow down.

He also traveled a little more and began some hobbies; the one I think he was most proud of was his garden. Countless vegetables and many fruit trees were cultivated by him. He reminded me of Grandpa Calvano growing all those leafy green things in his backyard. His trips to San Diego with Aunt Gloria to visit us were frequent until a few years before he died.

Uncle Gene and Aunt Gloria were deeply committed to God and the teachings of Jesus Christ. One of his constant lines when about to make a point was "If you believe in the teachings of Jesus Christ" you will do this or that. He truly believed. When they stayed at our home I would find them early in the morning each reading their prayer books. They always found the convenient mass to attend and most always left before Sunday so he could say the readings at mass in the church in Apple Valley.

Back to the cars for a moment. Those big Caddies, Olds, and Pontiacs weren't just luxury cars to me. They represented the strength of the man. They represented leadership, dreams, and abilities to make things happen too. As he got older and the cars got smaller, he never lost the strength, the leadership, dreams or the ability to make things happen.

This man overcame his own fears, charted his own course and got things done.

Was he an elitist? Perhaps somewhat. Was he opinionated? Yes. Was he pushy? Sometimes. Did he mind other people's business? Sometimes too much. Was he compassionate? Very much.

Did he love his wife and kids? Yes, completely. Did he love the rest of his family? Yes, without a doubt. Did he believe in people? Yes. Did he believe in himself? Absolutely. Could he make decisions? YES!

Did he believe in the love of God and Jesus Christ? Probably more than anything else.

Was he human? Yes, and with all the power and frailties that any man could have.

All of my uncles were cool men. Uncle Pepe, soft spoken and patient. I still think of him when I back out of a driveway because he taught me how to do it in my Bonneville. Uncle Bussy's mechanical prowess saved me a few times in that same

Bonneville and many family members as well. Uncle Art. Now there was one cool dude who could build anything and cook like a chef. What was it about Uncle Gene that made me want to follow him even though he really didn't cook much, never built anything, couldn't fix his cars, and at times was not very patient?

Here's the answer: many years ago, I was involved in a deal in which I felt I was being taken advantage of. When I told Uncle Gene the circumstances of the deal he asked me what I thought was right for me. I told him and he said make them the same offer. I said I couldn't because I didn't have the funding. He said, "Now you do, I'll lend you the money." The deal was successfully completed. So the answer to the question is very simple. Uncle Gene had strength to make the deal, strength to follow through on his commitments, strength to forgive and strength to be humble.

What a man!

By Rose Ann Rasic

My family has always been a main force in my life. My earliest memories are of parties—christenings, First Communions, showers, weddings, birthdays or delicious Sunday dinners—anything was an excuse to be together and celebrate.

Memories of those times are powerful—a certain song, especially one played by the "Ritz Brothers" (that's what my dad and uncles called their band) or sung by Auntie Ida; the smell of Italian cheese or spaghetti sauce; the sound of my large family laughing and playing—all remind me of my childhood, of my heritage.

I'm the fifth oldest of 24 grandchildren, one of the "big kids" who was supposed to be kind of in charge of the younger ones. But that role never came naturally to me; instead, I wanted to hang with the grown-ups, especially my aunts and uncles whom I adored. My dad's three brothers—Art, Al and Gene—were full of fun and mischief but also excellent role models of how to be a strong person, work hard, be respectful, etc.

My two Calvano aunts and three uncles, plus my dad, grew up in the South Side of Chicago, in the days when ethnicities had their own territories, married within their nationalities and clung to tradition.

Uncle Gene, the youngest, always shone in my eyes. He was handsome (as they all were), with dark hair and eyes, a warm smile and a sharp mind. When the brothers talked about their youth, we kids couldn't get enough details. The famous/infamous story of who got the big tip for selling a newspaper to Al Capone is family legend. (We're still not sure who the lucky boy was!). But there were plenty of anecdotes about the rougher times, mostly because money was tight and the kids had to drop out of school to help support the family.

Some of it was urban legend, no doubt, but there was always a grain of truth to these stories. Uncle Gene didn't finish high school, yet he became a top executive with Safeway Stores, working himself up the ladder and eventually managing the western United States produce department. Quite an accomplishment, and we were all so proud.

But he was more than an executive. Deep down, he was a religious, loving family man. He always cited his mother as the major influence in his life, she of the twinkling blue eyes and ready smile, she who loved teaching us how to cook and bake and be Italian. He carried on that tradition in his family, frequently talking of the wise words that Grandma passed along.

When Uncle Gene married Aunt Gloria (a beautiful, kind, sweet woman), I was about 12 years old, just at the age to be romantically smitten with the wedding and all of the preparations. My family lived in one room behind Grandma and Grandpa at that time (this was quite an adventure for DeDe and me), so we were very close to the excitement.

We heard the women planning the food, talking about the dresses, the flowers. It was a lovely wedding, simple yet beautiful with familiar touches since the family participated fully.

Always close not just emotionally but physically, at one time five families lived on Duncannon Avenue in Duarte, and Grandma and Grandpa lived on the next block. I loved it! Cousins were always available for company and playing. My Aunt Theresa and Grandma taught me how to sew. Mom was an amazing cook (along with many others) and our house was the gathering place, especially after Dad and the uncles completed a screened-in patio almost half the size of our house! Many lively parties took place there, including one when Uncle Gene (the ringleader) and Uncle Art actually sprayed the garden hose full force in our kitchen! One of the few times I saw my mom get upset, but she quickly forgave the nonsense, as usual blaming it on too many beers.

Uncle Gene and Aunt Gloria had four beautiful kids, and as some of the older cousins DeDe and I often babysat when they lived directly across the street. Quite a handful for two pre-teens, but we had a great time spoiling them (don't tell Aunt Gloria). She was a meticulous housekeeper so we had to carefully put everything back before the kids went to bed—restore calm and order to chaos.

For many of the years that Uncle Gene was climbing the corporate ladder I was probably unaware of how great his accomplishment really was. He traveled a lot, went to important meetings, seems stressed often—a typical Type A before we knew what that was. At a particularly sad time in the family's history, he and Aunt Gloria became the guardians of Uncle Al's six kids and Uncle carried out that responsibility with his usual mix of discipline, dedication and diligence.

As I grew up, I began to realize just how much Uncle Gene could do, juggling more than anyone else in the family, I admired him and, looking back, I know that his attitude, faith and hard work were things I tried to emulate as I started a family of my own. With four young children soon under our roof, I appreciated more than ever the effort that goes into creating a strong marriage and family.

I was a stay-at-home mom for years, but always yearned for the college degree that I had aspired to in high school. At that time, it wasn't considered important or even necessarily okay for a Calvano cousin to go to college. We would work hard, have families, carry on traditions. All well and good, but our oldest cousin Maryann broke the mold when she started taking college courses. I was so jealous! But also bogged down the kids, house, etc.

Eventually, when my youngest, Jim, started first grade, I enrolled in Glendale College. The reactions were mixed from *la familia*. My mom thought I should stay home, dad loved the idea and most of the others were silent on the topic. But Uncle Gene wasn't silent (he seldom was). He encouraged me and asked me why I was doing it and what I hoped to achieve. My response: It's just something I have to do, I want to learn. We shared that drive and that was the first time it had been expressed.

Perhaps the greatest influence Uncle Gene had on me was in my career. I had some interesting jobs with my English degree, from public relations to an anti-drunk drive campaign to traveling the world for the Hilton Foundation. I would never have believed it, growing up on Duncannon. My dreams of travel and adventure came true in a most unexpected way. I don't know if he ever realized it, but the fact that Uncle Gene started over a few times; he moved to the desert and built and operated a successful produce store; he managed a date farm in Indio; and eventually he learned finance and became more active in the Church. The fact that he was bold enough to learn new skills and take on new responsibilities at the ripe old age of 65 (or older) gave me the push and confidence I needed to take on jobs that previously had seemed beyond me. Working for the nonprofit, I traveled the U.S., meeting with politicians, bishops, educators and other leaders. I had the amazing opportunity to explore countries in Asia, Africa, South America and more as a consultant for the Hilton Foundation.

These adventures had never occurred to me, never seemed possible as I created a home and raised my children. But Uncle Gene understood—and shared—the restless curiosity that some of us cannot deny in ourselves. He was always learning, growing, and spreading his ideas. And through it all, until his last days, he put faith and family first. A life well lived, and one I hope I can emulate in these, my "golden years."

By DeDe (Calvano) Buechler

For as long as I can remember, Uncle Gene was an important part of my life. In fact, his own central role began before I had a memory, when he and Gramma Calvano attended the graveside service for my twin sister, Patricia, who died when she was three days old. My dad (Uncle Bussie) appreciated Uncle Gene's presence. At the time of the burial, my mom (Auntie Mary) was still hospitalized after having had a Caesarean section to deliver us. Already bereft at the death of my twin, she and my dad had yet another reason to mourn. Their dreams of having a large family, and especially the opportunity to try for a son were gone. Mom could carry no more children. So Uncle Gene became memorable before I knew him.

While my older sister, Rose Ann, and I were growing up, my family lived behind Gramma and Grampa Calvano until I went to school. Still single, Uncle Gene had plenty of time on his hands to spend with Rose Ann and me. We were very special to him as he had no children of his own.

One of our favorite playtimes with him was when he'd lift us to hang from a patio beam and then tell us to jump into his arms, so we did. We trusted him completely. I'm amazed Dad didn't object as he was very protective of both of his daughters, but he also trusted Uncle Gene.

Throughout his long life, Uncle Gene was at all of the family celebrations – baptisms, confirmations, birthdays, holidays, reunions – and funerals for close and extended family members. He always made me feel special and took an interest in my life.

He teased me a lot but would say, "I wouldn't tease you if I didn't love you." I knew he did it with love, and his razzing taught me to be a good sport later in life. After marrying Aunt Gloria, his life changed, of course, but not his love for his nieces.

Eventually, he and Aunt Gloria moved across the street from us in Duarte, Calif., three of the four Calvano brothers and their two sisters lived – all on the same block for some time. Gramma and Grampa were a block away.

Their family was young and still growing at the time, so Rose Ann and I often were called to babysit their four kids, which we enjoyed very much. He was careful about leaving the kids with just anyone, so asking us to babysit meant he trusted us. I remember taking Annie and Pete to the park when I got home from school. He thanked me for this frequently; he said it gave Aunt Gloria a break.

I can still picture him and Aunt Gloria sitting on the front porch steps of their house at night after the kids were in bed. I'm sure this was their special time together, and it always looked special to me.

My dad retired at age 45, the result of a severely injured back. Sometimes when my parents needed financial help, Uncle Gene was there to help. He never wanted recognition for his generosity. He helped out of love for his brother.

When I got married in 1972, he and Aunt Gloria paid for the food at my reception to relieve my parents of a potential financial hardship. (I don't think he told anyone in the family that he did this so as to not embarrass my folks.) That's the kind of man he was.

Even though I moved to Arizona after my marriage, Uncle Gene always kept in touch by visits or phone calls. After my dad passed away, he and Aunt Gloria visited my mom in Mesa, Ariz., many times, and they always came to see me as well. Mom had moved from California after Dad's death.

Uncle Gene was in management most of his life and would tell us stories about his employees and how he handled personnel problems. "Always respect your employees and they will respect you," he said. I made his philosophy my own throughout my career, and, in most circumstances, had a good relationship with those I supervised.

While at my first husband Bob's memorial service – Bob died eight days after Mom had – Uncle Gene spoke to some of my employees who were at the service. He told me they respected and liked working for me. That meant so much. Looking back, Uncle Gene was the only family member who was in management, so his sharing of his experiences carried me far.

He was a man of his word. For example, after Uncle Al fell from a tree and was critically injured and then died two months later, in 1966, Uncle Gene became the guardian of five of Uncle Al's six children. While I am sure this change of events wasn't easy for him and Aunt Gloria, they honored their promise to look after Uncle Al's children. What a tremendous responsibility for both of them.

I admire them for the sacrifice this took, which also emphasized the importance and meaning of "family" to me.

They demonstrated "family" to me, personally, when they'd come to see Mom several times in Arizona as her cancer progressed. With each visit, he would tell me I was doing a great job of watching over her; his encouragement strengthened me during a difficult time.

I always looked up to Uncle Gene for his caring ways and ability to understand my situation. After my mom's and Bob's deaths, I was devastated and didn't know whether I should move back to California. He suggested I think hard about the prospect of moving and pray about it because I already had good friends in Arizona, a job, and my church members were there for me, too. He also mentioned that I would be going through a grief process that would be difficult. Relocating could make my time of mourning even more difficult, he said.

My emotions were raw then, and I was baffled about what to do next. But his words stayed with me. For example, in Arizona, he said, I would have sunshine most of the year, an advantage during my depression and that I would need to find another job in California. At the time, I was in no condition emotionally to look for different work.

Uncle Gene always said he would pray for me, and at that time, I needed his prayers very much. After my mom's death, he would call frequently to check in, which deeply touched me.

I met Allan Buechler in 1990 and took him to a cousin's wedding. We hadn't been dating long, but when I introduced him to Uncle Gene, he said, "DeDe, you have good judgment," and to Allan, "so I'm sure you are a good man." He is a good man and has been a good husband for 27 years.

Uncle Gene and Aunt Gloria came to our wedding and I asked him to say grace before the meal. I so missed my parents, but he did his best to fill in for them.

Allan and I attended Uncle Gene and Aunt Gloria's 50th and 60th anniversary parties, and I was honored to participate in the celebration. I always looked forward to seeing him at the family reunions, and when he passed away, he was so missed. I didn't always agree with his views but respected them, and always felt respected by him.

Throughout his life, Uncle Gene emphasized the importance of faith and prayer. His faith meant everything to him. Even though my path took a turn away from the Catholic Church and toward a Protestant one, my faith remains strong, and I remembered his words, especially in my most difficult moments. He never preached to me about leaving the Catholic Church and was happy I had found a church family elsewhere.

He was a humble man of faith throughout his life. I was very lucky to have him in my life for so many years. He was a leader in our family and could be counted on to be there for us, no matter the circumstances.

Uncle Gene, you are loved and missed.

Love, DeDe

By Rita Calvano Smith

He was Unc and I was Reet. In the face of great tragedy, he took us under his wing, with Aunt Gloria beside him, and they loved us. He trusted my judgment, gave me huge family responsibilities and assumed guardianship of five of the six of us children nearly fifty years ago.

Through the years, Unc would remind us of his own responsibility. "I promised your dad I would take care of you guys, and I'm going to live up to that promise," he said periodically.

Recently, he told me in good humor why he'd agreed. "Your dad pestered and pestered me to take care of you in case something happened to him. I got so sick of hearing him that finally I said, 'Okay, goddamn it, I will!'"

Indeed he did, propping us up through the shock and resultant turmoil of the deaths of our parents; lecturing us on our responsibilities through our thorny teenage years; advising us as we became young adults still in need of guidance; encouraging and respecting us for our efforts, and acknowledging his pride at whom we'd become.

For me personally, he was a beacon of hope, common sense, encouragement and humor as I struggled to do or say the right thing. As a 19-year-old taking care of a household with four minors, including myself, in our own apartment, I counted on his wisdom, fortitude, determination, to help us recover from the countless shocks in our early lives so that we would become generous, compassionate, happy adults.

He never failed me, not once, despite our occasional disagreements, the heaviest of which was his belief in God and my lack of one. As we grew up, and Unc's beliefs grew ever deeper and his religious practices more frequent and fervent, I once wrote him that I didn't want to hurt his feelings, but his preaching became too much at times for me to handle. It made me anxious, and I felt judged.

He called after reading my note to say, "Reet, I think I owe you an apology."

That was Gene Calvano.

Of course, when one believes as strongly as he did, it's difficult to curb that enthusiasm.

"You need to pray to God for strength."

"Unc, I don't have a god," I'd say, "and I don't pray."

He assured me that that was all right and just to do whatever I do to find answers. "Read a book, take deep breaths, whatever you do," he'd say. "I'll send you a book that I have that might help you. It has some religious overtones, but it mostly has good advice," he'd say. I read them all, still have them.

This story is hard to tell. It's very personal and I might be harshly judged by some, and shunned. But the point is, he and I left room in our hearts for the other. Gene Calvano was about acceptance and example. We respected and loved each other, anyway, and learned from one another.

"I could belong to any church. I am a Christian and believe in the teachings of Jesus Christ. It happens that I'm Catholic," he said.

Those teachings involved loving others: by sharing ourselves and our wealth, financial or otherwise, even when it stretches our limits but not so much that we can't take care of ourselves; by visiting the lonely, sick or not; giving a ride to somebody without one; lending an ear; sharing a meal — by anticipating the needs of others. Our duty was to think and act beyond ourselves. By way of example, he took Communion to the sick for ten years, retiring from one of his many kindly endeavors only weeks ago because walking the halls of a hospital for four hours a week became too physically strenuous: His legs swelled.

This acceptance and all of the other virtues I've attached to him made him a man of the world. So the world has lost a good friend, a statesman, not in the political sense, but in life, a man who would spcak up for what he believed, to a parish council; a Safeway produce manager whose displays needed dressing up; a niece – many nieces, nephews, other family members, acquaintances, if he thought they needed guidance.

He called on every birthday, Auntie Gloria sent cards, and they touched my bashful husband, enabling him to enjoy an occasional family meal when they came to town to visit all of us. And the two of them cupped my broken heart when my husband died last year, calling, encouraging, guiding me to salve the deep wound from my loss.

Now, I have another deep wound, and don't quite know how to heal it. But I'll remember the privilege of having been loved by and loving him. I will practice what he preached. Such a rich life he led and shared.

He was Unc, and I was Reet.

Glo, you were his angel; Annie, Dom and Mary, he constantly sang your praises and Pete's. Thank you for sharing him even at times when I'm certain you wanted him for yourselves.

Just so that others don't feel excluded, Unc loved our large Calvano family, his grandchildren and great-grandchildren and admired the accomplishments of all of you – and so many others he'd met during his 92 years.

How could we not miss his love.

And for those of us of the persuasion, his Democratic votes.

PHOTO SECTION

Rita
and
Clifford
Smith

Annie
and
Ed
Gaunder

Ladies and Gentlemen
Gene and Gloria Calvano

The Experts

SAFEWAY

to sophisticated, knowledgeable Los Angeles grocery shoppers. Step one was to ask the Division's ad agency, Ralph Kent Cooke, Inc., for a complete analysis of competitive campaigns, with particular emphasis on the various factors that seemed important to the people actually shopping in stores: ours and competitors'. What turns them on and off? How do they respond to jingles, promises of low, low prices, powerfully stated claims for superior selection, quality and service? Not surprisingly, it turned out that today's shopper *appreciates and will listen to honest, direct presentations that lead to logical conclusions about the things most important in developing a supermarket shopping habit: products, prices, services and so on.* It was also evident that such messages are best delivered by people who logically should know what they are talking about—people whose knowledge is evident and accurate.

Technical Problem: Translate this information into a new and interesting viewpoint of Safeway's special competitive advantages, using TV as the prime medium. The appropriate advantages were isolated by the Division's advertising people, and the agency's creative people went to work. Ideas were screened, developed, discarded. Some campaigns were almost completely developed on paper before they were dropped by the wayside; bright, shiny, clever campaigns that fit the problem and might have done the job but fell just short of being unmemorable, unique and convincing. "Back," kept saying Cal Gunnell, our Los Angeles Advertising Manager, "to the old drawing board."

Solution: The development of a simple idea; one that measured up to Safeway standards for honesty, believability, memorability and uniqueness.

According to Gunnell, "It may sound a little immodest, but when you get right down to the nitty-gritty, nobody knows more about food, and shopping, than Safeway people . . . we're the experts. The EXPERTS. That one word provided the key for an entire campaign."

SAFEWAY NEWS, OCTOBER 1974

VOICE: This is what I look for in a pineapple . . . fresh green leaves on the crown . . . a golden color that's tinged with green and see these little points? They're called pips and when they start to separate, the flavor is just right. I can tell you where you'll always find pineapple like this one . . . at Safeway and I have to know what I'm talking about. I work for Safeway.

CLOSING TAG:
If you're gonna buy fruits and vegetables, buy from people who know 'em best . . . the experts at Safeway.

VOICE: This is what a Grade AA Egg should look like. No cracks or pin holes and a thick, smooth shell. A thin, rough shell means air can affect freshness and flavor. This egg was sprayed with a food grade mineral oil to seal the shell, quality and freshness. That's what I have to look for. And I see more eggs in one day than most people see in a lifetime. I work for Safeway.

CLOSING TAG:
If you're gonna buy eggs, buy from people who know 'em best . . . the experts at Safeway.

Left:
Battlefield at Peleiu

Gene Calvano

"Gramma" With Her Entourage

Left to Right"
Gene, Art, Rose, Al and Dominick

Peter Calvano Family

Top Row: Dusti Jo, Thomas, Stefani
Bottom Row: Pete Calvano, Thomas, Ying

Thomas and Christopher Calvano

Gene Calvano
and brother
Al Calvano

Gene Calvano
and sister
Theresa Griffo

Left to Right:
Gloria Calvano, Mary Calvano, Dom Calvano, Annie Calvano, Gene Calvano, Pete Calvano

Left to Right:
Mary Garcea, Gloria Calvano, Gene Calvano

Gloria Calvano

The Dominick Calvano Family

Top Left: Dom and Kirstien

Courtney

Kristi-Lynn and Anthony

Misty, Dom, Mandy and Seth

Gene
Calvano

Mother Rose
Gene Calvano
Father Sam

The Dittemore's

Left to Right Back Row: Daryn Dittemore, Justin Dittemore, Alisa Dittemore,
David Dittemore, Gabby Dittemore, Tami Dittemore, Faye Barber, Larry Barber,
Gracie Bella Barber,
Left to Right Front Row: Kayleigh Dittemore, Bryanna Dittemore, Mary Dittemore,
Pete Dittemore, Ethan Dittemore, Anthony Dittemore, Caleb Barber

Left to Right:
Kristi-Lynn Lake
Dom Calvano
Mandy Calvano

This is the Altar that Gene Calvano Built for Christmas
on Peleliu Island

Palelau
Dad made
alter from flatbead
three Christmas Eve
Dad in chair

The Gene Calvano Family

Annie, Pete, Gene, Gloria, Dom and Mary

Brother Al - on Accordian
Brother Art - on Sax

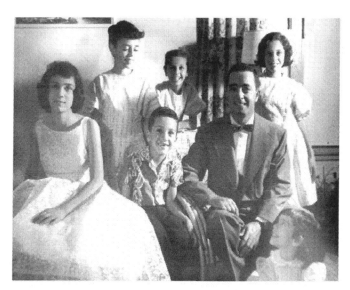

Front Row: Jennie, Sam, Uncle Al
Back Row: Rosie, Joni and Rita

Sam and Loyda Calvano

Christine Calvano

Back row: Jeane, Joni, Rosie, Christine, Sam
Front row: Rita, Gene, Gloria

Sam and Joni Halpern

Judy Pepe and
Christine Calvano

Annie, Rosie and Christine

Gloria and Gene Calvano

Gene and Gloria's Wedding Day
Delores Garcea (Gloria's sister), Gloria, Gene, Dominick
and Jeanne

The alter Gene helped build at Peleliu

Sister, Ida Pepe
and
Gene Calvano

Dominick Calvano (Busse)
Gene Calvano (Ray)

The Making of an Ad Campaign...

TV production session looks disorganized, but it isn't. Each person, a specialist, takes care of special job and then compromises through director.

ADVERTISING people are, contrary to the "glamour" image created by novelists, not unlike other business people. True, they may have lunch on a TV production stage instead of in the company cafeteria; true, they sometimes associate with artists, performers and other creative people whose names are widely known; true, their working hours are frequently irregular and totally flexible. But basically, advertising people are just like all the rest of us who try to do a job as well as we can. An exact similarity between the work of advertising people and that of warehousemen, accountants, retail managers and messengers is that each, in order to do the job properly, must find ways to be increasingly useful and efficient.

It's a never-ending problem for all of us, and for advertising folks it arises primarily when it appears that a new and different approach is required to achieve changing marketing goals. This article will take you backstage to see how new campaigns are conceived and produced.

Scene: Los Angeles, a vast market with several highly competitive supermarkets, each of which has solid, dynamic advertising working for it. Safeway's two-fold problem was to develop advertising which would stand apart (and above) the crowd and which would carry conviction and credibility

SAFEWAY NEWS, OCTOBER, 1974

The Schlosser Family | Jeremy, Tiffini, Cody, Alex & Camy

Left to Right: Pat Schlosser, Ruth Schlosser, Shannon Schlosser, Travis Schlosser, Annie Gaunder, Trevor Schlosser, Dominick Schlosser, Ed Gaunder, Kristi Schlosser, Justin Schlosser, Dom Schlosser, John Gaunder, Denise Torres

Rose Calvano
and
Mary Calvano

Gene Calvano

Gene Calvano and one of his many produce stands

The Schwartz Family

Abby, Josh, Robbie, Noah, Madison
Stefani and Byron

Dusti Jo and Thomas

Left to right:
Dominick Calvano, Arthur Calvano, Alfred Calvano

46699271R00106

Made in the USA
Middletown, DE
31 May 2019